Williams v. Simonson

Trial Version

Second Edition

WILLIAMS V. SIMONSON

Trial Version

Second Edition

Anthony J. Bocchino

David A. Sonenshein

NITA®

NATIONAL INSTITUTE FOR TRIAL ADVOCACY

Address inquiries to:
Reprint Permission
National Institute for Trial Advocacy
1685 38th Street, Suite 200
Boulder, CO 80301-2735
Phone: (800) 225-6482
Fax: (720) 890-7069
Email: permissions@nita.org

ISBN 978-1-60156-553-2
eISBN 978-1-60156-554-9

FBA 1553

Printed in the United States of America

Wolters Kluwer

Official co-publisher of NITA.
WKLegaledu.com/NITA

CONTENTS

Introduction

1. The parties to this case are Mary Anne Williams, the Plaintiff, and David A. Simonson, Christine Jefferson, Nita University, and The Patterson Institute, the co-defendants.

2. This case includes gender discrimination and defamation claims based on a claim by the Plaintiff that she was denied tenure with the Defendant Nita University when she terminated a sexual relationship with the Defendant Simonson. She also claims gender discrimination based on a sexual harassment claim against Defendant Simonson.

3. This case file is designed for advanced advocacy training and involves difficult legal and factual issues for jury resolution. It also requires the examination of expert witnesses.

4. The parties have stipulated that all documents are authentic and meet the requirements of the Original Documents Rule. Other requirements for admissibility must be established by offering counsel.

5. This case file is completely fictitious and any resemblance to any person living or dead is coincidental and should not be misconstrued.

6. Please note that all years in the fictional, narrative portions of these materials are stated in the following form:

   YR-0 indicates the actual year in which the case is being tried (i.e., the present year);

   YR-1 indicates the preceding year (please use the actual year);

   YR-2 indicates the next preceding year (please use the actual year); et cetera.

   True, Gregorian-calendar years are used in citations to actual court cases and where actual historical events are described.

7. Note: Electronic versions of the exhibits are available for download here:

   http://bit.ly/1P20Jea

   Password: Williams2

IN THE UNITED STATES DISTRICT COURT
FOR THE DISTRICT OF NITA

MARY ANNE WILLIAMS Plaintiff v. DAVID A. SIMONSON, CHRISTINE JEFFERSON, NITA UNIVERSITY, and THE PATTERSON INSTITUTE Defendants	: : : : : : : : : : : : :	CIVIL ACTION NO. YR-1-1414 JURY TRIAL DEMANDED

COMPLAINT

PARTIES

1. Plaintiff, Mary Anne Williams, is a female, adult individual, who is a citizen of Nita and of the United States. She resides in Nita City, Nita.

2. (a). Defendant, David A. Simonson, is an adult individual, who is a citizen of Nita and of the United States. He resides in Nita City, Nita.

2. (b). Defendant, David A. Simonson, at all material times in this lawsuit, was the Director of the Defendant Patterson Institute, and an agent of the Defendant, Patterson Institute.

3. (a). Defendant, Christine Jefferson, is an adult individual, who is a citizen of Nita and of the United States. She resides in Nita City, Nita.

3. (b). Defendant, Christine Jefferson, at all material times in this lawsuit, was the Dean of the Nita University School of Public Policy, and an agent of the Defendant, Nita University.

4. (a). Defendant, Nita University, is a not-for-profit corporation, organized under the laws of the State of Nita, with its central office and School of Public Policy located in Nita City, Nita.

4. (b). Defendant, Nita University, is an employer within the meaning of Title VII of the Civil Rights Act of 1964, as amended, in that it engages in an industry affecting commerce and has had fifteen (15) or more employees for each working day in each of twenty (20) or more calendar weeks in the current or pending calendar year.

5. (a). Defendant, Patterson Institute, is a not-for-profit corporation, organized under the laws of Nita, with its place of business located in Nita City, Nita.

5. (b). Defendant, Patterson Institute, is an employer within the meaning of Title VII of the Civil Rights Act of 1964, as amended, in that it engages in an industry affecting commerce and has had fifteen (15) or more employees for each working day in each of twenty (20) or more calendar weeks in the current or pending calendar year.

JURISDICTION AND VENUE

6. Plaintiff invokes this Court's jurisdiction pursuant to 28 U.S.C. Section 1331, 42 U.S.C. Section 2000e-5(f)(3) and invokes Supplemental Jurisdiction pursuant to 28 U.S.C. Section 1367. This action arises pursuant to 42 U.S.C. Section 2000e et seq., Title VII of the Civil Rights Act of 1964, as amended.

7. All conditions precedent to the filing of this action have been satisfied in that the U.S. Equal Employment Opportunity Commission of the United States issued its right to sue notice on December 28, YR-2.

8. Venue is appropriate in the District of Nita because the Defendants reside or are incorporated in the State of Nita, the claims arose in the State of Nita, and the Defendants may be served with process there.

Claim I
Violation of the Civil Rights Act of 1964
Gender Discrimination

9. Plaintiff holds a BA Degree in Public Policy from Northwestern University, and a Ph.D. Degree in Public Policy from Duke University.

10. In July of YR-8, Defendant Nita University hired Plaintiff as an Assistant Professor in the School of Public Policy, where Plaintiff worked for six years before having her employment terminated. In January of YR-5, Plaintiff made a complaint to the University Committee on Discrimination regarding sexual harassment by Dean Richard Dressler, of the Business School of the Defendant Nita University.

11. During the time of her employment at the Defendant Nita University, Plaintiff was supervised by Defendant Jefferson.

12. During the time of her employment at the Defendant Patterson Institute, Plaintiff was supervised by Defendant Simonson.

13. In July of YR-4, Defendant Simonson, who was Plaintiff's supervisor at the Defendant Patterson Institute, initiated a sexual relationship with the Plaintiff, while she was working for him on the business of Defendant Nita University and Defendant Patterson Institute.

14. In January of YR-2, Plaintiff terminated her sexual relationship with Defendant Simonson, even though Defendant Simonson attempted to pressure her to continue that relationship and Defendant Jefferson was made aware of Plaintiff's actions by the Defendant Simonson.

15. Although Plaintiff received a positive vote for tenure, from the tenurial faculty of the School of Public Policy of the Defendant Nita University, and was qualified for tenure pursuant to the regulations of the Defendant Nita University, Plaintiff was not recommended for tenure by the Defendant Jefferson, and not granted tenure by the Defendant Nita University, while a male professor of a lower academic rank and less qualifications of the faculty of the School of Public Policy of the Defendant Nita University, was recommended for tenure by the Defendant Jefferson and granted tenure by the Defendant Nita University.

16. Plaintiff was not recommended for tenure by the Defendant Jefferson and not granted tenure by the Defendant Nita University, because she complained of sexual harassment by Richard Dressler in YR-5 and because she terminated a sexual relationship with the Defendant Simonson, in violation of Title VII of the Civil Rights Act of 1964, as amended.

Claim II
Violation of the Civil Rights Act of 1964
Quid Pro Quo Sexual Harassment—Retaliation

17. Plaintiff incorporates by reference Paragraphs 1–16, all of which amount to quid pro quo sexual harassment, retaliation, in violation of Title VII of the Civil Rights Act of 1964, as amended.

Claim III
Violation of the Civil Rights Act of 1964
Hostile Work Environment

18. Plaintiff incorporates by reference Paragraphs 1–16.

19. Defendant Nita University, through its policies allowed the maintenance of a hostile work environment wherein senior faculty members were not prevented from entering into sexual relations with junior faculty members on whose tenure the senior faculty members were allowed to vote and have potential negative influence, and through its policies allowed male employees to sexually harass female employees, all of which created and imposed on Plaintiff a hostile work environment in violation of Plaintiff's rights pursuant to Title VII of the Civil Rights Act of 1964, as amended.

20. Defendant Patterson Institute, through its policies, allowed the maintenance of a hostile work environment wherein its agent, Defendant Simonson, was allowed to have sexual relations with an employee, over whose employment he had complete control, all of which created and imposed on Plaintiff a hostile work environment in violation of Plaintiff's rights pursuant to Title VII of the Civil Rights Act of 1964, as amended.

WHEREFORE, Plaintiff prays that this Court will:

A. Issue a declaratory judgment declaring that the actions of the Defendants and all of them, as set forth in this Complaint, violated Plaintiff's rights pursuant to Title VII of the Civil Rights Act of 1964, as amended.

B. Enjoin and restrain Defendants, and all of them, and all other persons acting on behalf of, or in concert with them, from engaging in such unlawful conduct.

C. Enter judgment in favor of Plaintiff, and against Defendants Nita University and Patterson Institute, for back pay in the amount of wages and fringe benefits it is determined that Plaintiff lost as a result of Defendants' unlawful conduct, together with interest.

D. Enter judgment in favor of Plaintiff and against Defendants Nita University and Patterson Institute, reinstating the Plaintiff to the positions of:

1. Associate Professor with tenure in the School of Public Policy of Defendant Nita University; and

2. Associate Director of Defendant Patterson Institute, which she would have attained absent Defendants' unlwaful conduct. In the alternative, award Plaintiff front pay in the amount of wages and benefits that Plaintiff is likely to lose because of Defendants' unlawful conduct.

E. Enter judgment in favor of Plaintiffs, and against Defendants and all of them, for compensatory damages, including but not limited to, damages for physical pain, mental anguish, humiliation, economic losses other than wages and medical expenses, together with interest.

F. Award Plaintiff reasonable attorney's fees together with the costs of this litigation.

G. Award such other and further legal and equitable relief as may be appropriate to redress fully the deprivation of Plaintiff's rights, to prevent their recurrence in the future, and to protect other employees of Defendant Nita University and Defendant Patterson Institute from such unlawful behavior.

Claim IV
Intentional Infliction of Emotional Distress

21. Plaintiff incorporates Paragraphs 1–16 by reference.

22. The actions of Defendant Simonson and Defendant Jefferson, as set forth above, were malicious, willful, wanton, outrageous in the extreme, intolerable in a civilized society, and specifically calculated to cause serious mental distress to the Plaintiff and requiring professional psychological and medical intervention.

23. The actions and omissions of Defendant Nita University in ratifying the acts of Defendant Jefferson and Defendant Simonson, and the actions and omissions of the Defendant Patterson Institute in ratifying the acts of the Defendant Simonson, as set forth above were malicious, willful,

wanton, outrageous in the extreme, intolerable in a civilized society, and specifically calculated to cause serious mental distress to the Plaintiff and requiring professional psychological and medical intervention.

Claim V
Wrongful Termination

24. Plaintiff incorporates by reference Paragraph 1–16

WHEREFORE, Plaintiff demands judgment against Defendants, and all of them, for compensatory damages in excess of $75,000, including but not limited to, damages for physical pain, mental anguish, humiliation, loss of the joys of life, loss of earnings and other loss, economic losses and punitive damages in an amount reasonably calculated to punish Defendants and all of them for their actions as stated above, together with interest and costs of suit.

Claim VI
Defamation

25. Plaintiff incorporates by reference Paragraphs 1–16.

26. Following Plaintiff's termination from employment at Defendant Nita University and Defendant Patterson Institute, Plaintiff applied for positions on the faculty of over one hundred (100) Universities, including Columbus University of Conwell and Nita State University.

27. Defendant Simonson, as the Director of the Defendant Patterson Institute and Defendant Jefferson Dean of the School of Public Policy of the Defendant Nita University, maliciously provided statements in letters to the aforementioned prospective employers that were false and slanderous with regard to Plaintiff's professional qualifications.

28. The statements of the Defendant Simonson were made with the express, implied, or apparent authority of the Defendant Patterson Institute and thereby ratified by the Defendant Patterson Institute.

29. The statements of the Defendant Jefferson were made with the express, implied, or apparent authority of the Defendant Nita University and thereby ratified by the Defendant Nita University.

30. As a result of the aforementioned statements and ratifications as stated in Paragraphs 27, 28, and 29, Plaintiff has suffered substantial emotional distress, mental anguish, and pain and suffering; as well as damage to her personal and professional reputation and earning capacity

WHEREFORE, Plaintiff demands judgment against Defendants, and all of them, for compensatory and punitive damages in an amount in excess of $1,000,000.

JURY DEMAND

Plaintiff demands a jury trial for all claims triable by way of Jury.

Respectfully submitted,

Charles R. Twiggs, Esq.
One Constitution Plaza
Conwell City, Conwell

Dated: December 28, YR-1

VERIFICATION

I, Mary Anne Williams, am the Plaintiff in the above captioned action. I have read the complaint and verify that the allegations contained, herein are true.

Mary Anne Williams

Signed and sworn before me,
this 28th day of December, YR-1.

Notary Public

IN THE UNITED STATES DISTRICT COURT
FOR THE DISTRICT OF NITA

MARY ANNE WILLIAMS	:	
Plaintiff	:	CIVIL ACTION NO.
	:	YR-1-1-1414
v.	:	JURY TRIAL DEMANDED
	:	
DAVID A. SIMONSON,	:	
	:	
CHRISTINE JEFFERSON,	:	
	:	
NITA UNIVERSITY,	:	
and	:	
	:	
THE PATTERSON INSTITUTE	:	
Defendants	:	

**ANSWER OF DEFENDANTS
AND COUNTERCLAIM OF DEFENDANT, SIMONSON**

By way of answer, Defendants David A. Simonson, Christine Jefferson, Nita University and Patterson Institute, respond to Plaintiff's allegations as follows:

1. Admit

2. (a) Admit

2. (b) Admit

3. (a) Admit

3. (b) Admit

4. (a) Admit

4. (b) Admit

5. (a) Admit

5. (b) Admit

6. Admit

7. Admit

8. Admit

9. Admit

10. Admit

11. Admit

12. Admit

13. Deny that the sexual relationship was initiated by Defendant Simonson. The relationship was mutually, freely, and willingly entered into by the Plaintiff and Defendant Simonson. Plaintiff was an employee of Defendant Patterson Institute. The sexual relationship was not entered into while Plaintiff was working on the business of the Patterson Institute.

14. Admit that Plaintiff terminated the sexual relationship with the Defendant Simonson. Deny all other allegations in this paragraph.

15. Admit that Plaintiff received a positive vote for tenure by a vote of 15–12 with one abstention from the Tenurial Faculty of the Nita University School of Public Policy. Admit that Plaintiff was not recommended for tenure by Defendant Jefferson. Admit that Plaintiff was not granted tenure by the Defendant Nita University. Deny all other allegations in this paragraph.

16. Denied

17. Admit all allegations already admitted and deny all allegations already denied. Deny allegation of quid pro quo sexual harrassment-retaliation.

18. Admit all allegations already admitted and deny all allegations already denied.

19. Denied

20. Denied

21. Admit all allegations already admitted and deny all allegation already denied.

22. Denied

23. Denied

24. Admit all allegations already admitted and deny all allegations already denied.

25. Admit all allegations already admitted and deny all allegations already denied.

26. Admit that Plaintiff applied for positions on University faculties. Defendants are without sufficient information to admit or deny the number of such applications.

27. Denied

28. Admit

29. Admit

31. Denied

Counterclaim

By way of counterclaim, Defendant David A. Simonson alleges the following:

1. Beginning in January of YR-2, following the termination of a consensual sexual relationship between the Plaintiff and the Defendant Simonson, Plaintiff made and continues to make false, slanderous, and malicious statements to members of the Nita University Faculty as well as to numerous other members of Defendant Simonson's profession, regarding Defendant Simonson's personal character and professional integrity, all of which caused the Defendant Simonson to suffer substantial emotional distress, mental anguish, and damage to his personal and professional reputation and earning capacity.

WHEREFORE, Defendant Simonson demands judgment against the Plaintiff, for compensatory and punitive damages in an amount in excess of $75,000.

Jury Demand

Defendants demand a jury trial for all claims triable by way of jury.

Respectfully submitted

Meredith Aquino

Meredith Aquino
Counsel for Defendants

Dated: January 15, YR-0

Verification

I, David A. Simonson, Defendant/Plaintiff-in-Counterclaim, in the above-captioned matter, have read the counterclaim complaint and verify that the allegations contained therein are true.

David A. Simonson

Signed and sworn before me, this 15th day of January, YR-0

Notary Public

IN THE UNITED STATES DISTRICT COURT
FOR THE DISTRICT OF NITA

MARY ANNE WILLIAMS Plaintiff v. DAVID A. SIMONSON. ET, AL:	: : : : : : : :	CIVIL ACTION NO. YR-1-1-1414 JURY TRIAL DEMANDED

REPLY TO COUNTERCLAIM

By way of reply to Defendant Simonson's counterclaim, Plaintiff responds as follows:

1. Denied. All statements made by Plaintiff regarding Defendant Simonson were and are true.

Respectfully submitted:

Charles R. Twiggs
Counsel for Plaintiff

MEMO TO PARTICIPANTS——

Elements of the Causes of Action Claimed by the Plaintiff in *Williams v. Simonson*

Gender Discrimination (Generally)

Plaintiff's Prima Facie Burden—

1. Plaintiff belongs to a protected class (female);
2. Plaintiff applied for a position with the Defendant;
3. Plaintiff was qualified for the position;
4. Despite qualifications she was not selected; and
5. After denial, the position remained open and Defendant sought male candidates for the position.

Once Plaintiff proves above,

Defendant has burden of showing legitimate, non-discriminatory purpose for failing to select Plaintiff.

If Defendant meets its burden, Plaintiff has the burden of showing that Defendant's purpose was a sham.

Gender Discrimination Quid Pro Quo

Plaintiff has burden to show—

1. She is a female;
2. She was an employee of Defendant;
3. She was the subject of unwanted sexual harassment by way of sexual advances or requests for sexual favors;
4. Her submission to such advances was a condition of employment or continued employment; and
5. Her refusal to enter into or continue in an unwanted sexual relationship was the cause of her loss of employment.

Gender Discrimination
Hostile Work Environment

1. She is female;

2. She was an employee of Defendant;

3. She was subjected to unwanted sexual harassment;

4. The harassment complaint was based on sex; and

5. The harassment complained of affected a term, condition, or privilege of employment.

Intentional Infliction of Emotional Distress

1. Defendant acted maliciously, willfully, wantonly, or outrageously in the extreme toward the Plaintiff;

2. Defendant committed an act intolerable in a civilized society;

3. Defendant committed an act specifically calculated to cause the Plaintiff serious mental distress;

4. The Plaintiff suffered serious mental distress.

Wrongful Discharge

1. Plaintiff was employed by Defendant;

2. Plaintiff was discharged or terminated by Defendant; and

3. The termination or discharge was for a reason or reasons which violated law and/or public policy.

Defamation

1. Defendant published a statement concerning the plaintiff;

2. The statement was defamatory, which means that if taken as a whole, the statement tends to harm the reputation of the Plaintiff as to lower her in the estimation of the community or to deter a third party from associating or dealing with her; and

3. The statement was false and unprivileged.

   There is qualified privilege for statements made by a present or former employer to a prospective employer of Plaintiff. This privilege is negated by malice on the part of the Defendant.

Deposition of Mary Anne Williams

My name is Mary Anne Williams. I am thirty-two years old and single. I live at 115 Winding Way in Nita City, Nita. I have lived at that address since June of YR-1. Before that I lived with my parents for a year at 85 Farm Hill Road in Wallingford, Conwell. Before that I had lived at various addresses in Nita City for the period of time from August YR-8 until July YR-2. My last address in Nita City was 45C Coventry Fields Condominiums. When I lost my job at Nita University in May YR-2, I had to sell my condo and I moved home to live with my parents while I looked for a new job. I now work as a researcher at the Beecher Institute in Nita City which is a political think tank and I teach part time at Nita Community College.

I did my undergraduate work at Northwestern University in Evanston, Illinois. I graduated in YR-11 with a BA in Public Policy. I then got my Ph.D. in Public Policy from the Duke University Sanford School of Public Policy in YR-8. I was hired as an Assistant Professor at the Nita University School of Public Policy in YR-8. All of this is reflected in my resume, which you just showed to me. (See Exhibit 2) David Simonson was the dean of the Public Policy School when I was hired. He recruited me and he was the primary reason I took the offer from Nita U over several other offers I had. Simonson was a nationally recognized expert in public policy, who was in his thirties at the time, and considered a rising star. He frequently testified before Congress and was a consultant to the White House on a number of occasions as well as serving on several Presidential Commissions. Exhibit 3 is the appointment letter I received from then Dean Simonson. Exhibit 1 is a copy of the tenure and promotion standards at the University that was enclosed in the appointment letter.

Within a month of my accepting the position at Nita U, Simonson stepped down as dean and assumed the position of director of the Patterson Institute for Public Policy. At the same time he was named the Patterson Professor of Public Policy. Both the Institute and the Patterson Chair were the result of a $10 million grant from the Patterson Foundation. I understand that Simonson was instrumental in bringing the Patterson grant to the University and is a personal friend of Gregory Patterson, Jr., Chair of the Board of the Patterson Institute, and a member of the Nita U Board of Trustees.

Beginning in YR-6 I also took on a position as a researcher at the Patterson Institute. Exhibits 5A–5D are my yearly appointment letters for that position. In that role I was employed by the Patterson Institute and my direct supervisor was David Simonson. He was the one who encouraged me to take the position and advised me that it would assist in advancing my career within the Public Policy School. He told me that through the Patterson Institute I could attract some grant money to the University and that was an important factor in advancement within the Public Policy School and the University. I was flattered by the offer. There were other young Public Policy School faculty members who were also interested in the position, but Simonson selected me. I was considered at that point in my career, a good teacher and my scholarship was acceptable, but in today's world, in order to be tenured in a public policy school it's almost necessary to be able to attract some grant money. That is especially true in a public University such as Nita U where government support for higher education is shrinking.

Because of my position at the Patterson Institute I was able to work closely with Professor Simonson. He and I coauthored several reports (although only his name appeared on them) and worked together on several grants. He and I spent a great deal of time together and first became friends. In the Summer of YR-4, our friendship and close professional contact led to a sexual relationship. Yes, I was aware that David was married and had children, but he told me he was unhappy in his relationship with his wife, Kathryn. Kathryn Simonson is a medical doctor who is on the faculty at the Franklin Hospital Medical School in Nita City. She is a cardiac thoracic surgeon. As David explained it, his wife was really married to her profession, and had little interest in him and what he did. He also told me that she had her share of extramarital affairs over the years and that they had a marriage of convenience, for the benefit of his children. He said that he was waiting for the right relationship with someone else and that he would then seek a divorce.

I was also aware that David had a reputation for having sexual relationships outside his marriage and further that he had been involved with other young women faculty members in both the Public Policy School and other schools within the University. I had been warned by a number of people about him, including Professor Marvin Taylor of the Public Policy School faculty. Professor Taylor was the dean of the school before David Simonson and was the most respected senior faculty member in the School. Professor Taylor, who was in his late fifties when I joined the Nita U faculty, had taken me under his wing and had been of great assistance to me in my teaching and in my early scholarship. I consider him a mentor and a friend.

Yes, I know that Professor Taylor is gay and I've heard that Simonson was the one who "outed" him when Simonson was angling for the deanship of the Public Policy School in YR-9. I don't know what effect that had on Professor Taylor stepping down as dean or how he feels about the whole episode. I do know that Professor Taylor is the most respected member of the Public Policy faculty, with the possible exception of Simonson, and that he's perfectly comfortable with his sexuality. He is in a long-term, monogamous relationship with a man named Howard McDonald. I have been a guest in their home many times. Professor Taylor is also one of the faculty advisors to the Gay and Lesbian Alliance on campus, and has been for as long as I can remember, dating back to YR-8.

I know that Professor Taylor respects Simonson as a public policy professional. He encouraged me to accept Simonson's offer to work as a researcher at the Patterson Institute and to work with Simonson whenever I could. He did warn me about Simonson's reputation as a sexual predator, but I was confident I could take care of myself. As it turned out I should have listened to Professor Taylor and avoided Simonson personally. I could have avoided all of the problems Simonson has caused me.

As I said, my relationship with Simonson began as a professional one in YR-6 when I joined the staff of the Patterson Institute. Before that I had a cordial relationship with him, but no real contact. Simonson was always away from campus, consulting or speaking, in my first two years at Nita U. He did visit several of my classes (he came unannounced and sat in the back of the classroom) in YR-7 and early YR-6 and told me he was favorably impressed. It was in the Fall of YR-6 that I started at the Patterson Institute. As I said I worked closely with Simonson on a number of his grants.

In the summer of YR-4 we were completing work on a grant the Institute received from the Department of Education on privatization of public schools in urban areas. As is typical, as the report deadline approached the hours were longer and David and I worked many hours in close contact that summer. I was single and not involved, and his wife and kids were spending the month of July at the Outer Banks of North Carolina, so he was unattached as well. By that time we had a good working relationship and I'd say we were friends as well. David and I are both physical people and it was not unusual for us to touch each other in a non-sexual way. I did not find the touching offensive in any way. As I said it was familiar, but not sexual.

We often times would have meals together. In June of YR-4 we ate most lunches together when David was in town, and some dinners as well because we often worked into the evening hours. In July it was unusual when we didn't have both lunch and dinner together. We mostly talked about work related matters but did talk about personal matters, usually over dinner and a glass of wine. I became aware of his unhappiness with his marriage. I was uncomfortable talking about that topic for several reasons. First, I had been warned by Professor Taylor that this was David's typical line, but second, I'll admit I was attracted to him, both intellectually and to a lesser extent physically. I was coming off a relationship that had ended badly in the Spring of YR-4 and the last thing I needed was another relationship with a married man. I really prefer not to get into that relationship. It was not with anyone in the University and really has nothing to do with this case. No, I will not divulge his name or the circumstances of the relationship. It's not anyone else's business.

The report and application for refunding on the Department of Education grant was due on August 1. We finished both the report and the refunding application on July 30 and sent it out by Nita Parcel Service that day. That night David insisted that we get dressed up and go to dinner at La Brac, a very fancy restaurant in downtown Nita City. After a wonderful dinner, and a little too much wine, one thing led to another and we ended up spending the night together at my apartment. If I had been smart I would have left it at a one night stand, but that began a relationship that lasted until the early winter of YR-2.

Almost immediately, David started talking about our being a long term couple. He told me I was exactly what he was looking for: someone who shared his academic interests and cared about him as well as my career. We met almost exclusively at my place. We also attended professional conferences together. Over the next year our relationship got stronger and stronger and we spent a lot of time together. We continued to work together on the Department of Education grant that was renewed for one year in September YR-4 and again for a year in September YR-3. The initial grant and the renewals were in the amount of approximately $450,000 annually to the University and the Patterson Institute. Even though David's name was on the grant as the principal investigator, I was the one who was primarily responsible for the research and reports, as well as the grant renewal applications. David encouraged me to work hard on that project and said that the next major grant would go in with both of our names on it and list me, along with him, as principal investigators. This would have been an important career step for me.

David told me he was going to leave Kathryn many times over the first year of our relationship, but said that he wanted to go through counseling with her, and later with the kids, to make sure the split up wasn't too traumatic for the children. He said that he doubted that Kathryn cared whether he lived or died. He did stay living in the family home, which is a beautiful old stone colonial on University Drive right near the campus, for appearance purposes, or so he said. He often said that he would miss that house, which was Kathryn's family home that she inherited from her grandparents. I'll admit that I was tiring of being the other woman, but when I asked David about progress towards his separation he would put me off, typically saying the time wasn't right for one reason on another. In hindsight I'm sure it was just a line, that I was silly to trust him.

Although we didn't publicize the relationship, I think it was common knowledge that we were involved. I know that Professor Taylor suspected it was going on because he talked to me in May YR-3 right after I was promoted to associate professor. Yes, Exhibit 6 is the letter I received regarding my promotion and my expected tenure vote in YR-2. Professor Taylor told me that I should be careful, especially because I was coming up for tenure in YR-2, and he was sure some people wouldn't like the fact that David and I were involved, and that if anything happened to my relationship with David, that David had a history of being vindictive towards his former lovers. I assured Professor Taylor that my relationship with David was a genuine one, but that if anything happened I was sure that David wouldn't hold it against me personally given the strength of our professional relationship. Professor Taylor knew of my work on the Department of Education school privatization study grants, but warned me that my name wasn't on that grant. I told him that David had assured me that our next new project would be submitted under both our names. Professor Taylor said that would be important for my tenure vote that was scheduled for May YR-2.

I also believed that David's wife, was aware of my relationship with her husband because, according to David, he had told her. That was in Fall YR-3. David also told me that he and Kathryn had entered into some counseling that I understood to be for the purpose of insuring a smooth separation with as little disruption for the children as possible. The children, Debbie and Steven were seventeen and fifteen years old respectively. Debbie was in her senior year of high school at the time and Steven was in the tenth grade. Again, according to David, the plan was for counseling to begin with he and Kathryn, and the children would be brought in as the process evolved. This was ongoing, again according to David, through the fall of YR-3 and into the early winter. I'll admit I was becoming inpatient with the process, but David kept assuring me that things would work out, and frankly our relationship was as close as ever. Between work, meeting at my apartment, and several business trip/conventions we went on together, I had no reason to suspect otherwise.

In the fall of YR-3 I was offered the associate director's position at the Patterson Institute. David, of course, had a lot to do with the appointment. Exhibit 7 is that appointment letter from David Simonson in his position as director. That appointment was to begin on July 1, YR-2 and carried with it a stipend of $24,000 over and above my University salary which in academic year YR-3–YR-2 was $70,000 (plus fringe benefits that are calculated at 27 percent of salary). In that same academic year, my stipend as a researcher at the Patterson Institute was $11,500. The only condition of that appointment was that I become tenured by the University in Spring YR-2. Given my teaching and publication record and the fact that I was working on grants that were bringing significant amounts of money to the University, and with the support of both David and Professor Taylor, I was confident of a positive tenure vote. Yes, Exhibits 4A–4E are my Yearly Reports. I received them in the regular course from Dean Jefferson. I do not dispute their accuracy.

As I said, I was confident of receiving tenure in YR-2. It is generally known within the Public Policy School that Simonson was the leader of the younger tenured faculty and Professor Taylor the leader of the more senior faculty. These two groups often disagreed on policy and Dean Jefferson often had to mediate between the two groups on academic and other matters. They were both well respected scholars, but their real power with the University came from their ability to attract donations and grant funds. Professor Taylor had substantial influence within the University because he was considered the best fund raiser among the faculty and with the alumni as well, as having attracted many research grants to the Public Policy School. Simonson's stature within the University was tied up with his history of obtaining government and other grants and the Patterson Institute and his relationship with Gregory Patterson who was a member of the Board of Trustees and responsible for several large grants to the University in addition to what he contributed to endow the Patterson Institute and the Patterson Chair.

At any rate, in light of the raise from the Institute, and that security of tenure I believed I should receive, I decided to purchase a condominium near campus. I bought a two bedroom, two bath unit at the Coventry Farms complex in early November YR-3. I overpaid a little for the unit ($185,000), but it was in the nicest part of the complex and it had a small, enclosed backyard. I used the second bedroom as a study where both David and I could work. The unit was also large enough (with a big kitchen and great room) for two people. David continued to spend time with me after I moved and even kept a computer of his own there so we could both work at the same time at home, if necessary, and we often talked about how the condo would work great for us after David was separated.

By Christmas, I was settled into my new home. The holiday was a little lonely in that David went away with his family for the week between Christmas and New Year's Day. I wasn't happy about it, but David said that he and Kathryn were going to talk to the kids about the separation while on vacation, and that the separation was close, so that appeased me. David also had a conference that he was at speaking at during the first week of January in Europe. I was very busy and probably wouldn't have gone anyway, but he didn't invite me. As it turned out, David took Kathryn with him, even though he never said anything to me about it at the time.

When David returned for the beginning of classes, he avoided spending any time with me. There was always one excuse or another and he'd send me comments on Institute projects by e-mail instead of coming down the hall to talk. We finally planned to have dinner at the condo about a week after the semester began in late January. At dinner, David was very quiet and I wasn't able to get him to loosen up. I sensed there was something wrong and pressed David about his manner and asked him whether he had talked to Kathryn and the children about the divorce and whether it was going to proceed as he had stated earlier. He just blurted out that he and Kathryn needed to stay together for the kids and that he wasn't going to separate from her.

I was in shock. He talked about how the counseling had not gone that well with the kids and how Kathryn had made it clear during counseling that the separation was what David wanted and that she wanted to stay married to him. He said he couldn't allow himself to become estranged from his children, but that he still loved me and wanted to continue our relationship, albeit less publicly. I was hurt and got very angry. There were some harsh words exchanged. I made it very clear that I would no longer be his mistress; that I never would have started up with him except for his lies; and that our relationship was over. He tried to calm me down, saying that we had a good thing going, but I would have nothing of it.

I felt betrayed and used and told him so. I also told him that he was the most dishonest person I had ever met, not just in our relationship but in his work. When he protested, I pointed out that I had done most of the work on the Department of Education grant for the past several years and that he had taken all of the credit. At that he got really angry, told me I should be mindful of who I was talking to, and that I was in a precarious position. He then stormed out of the condo.

The next several weeks were horrible. I was depressed. I was mad. I was confused. I know I was distracted from my work. I was unable to work on an article that I was supposed to publish with the *American Public Policy Review* that was based on my work on public school privatization in urban areas and missed a publication deadline. Yes, that article was eventually published in October YR-2. It's shown on my resume. I also know that I was subpar in my classes as well and my class evaluations at the end of the semester reflected that fact. I finally sought some professional help in late March YR-2 and was diagnosed by Dr. Rachel Johnson, who is a psychologist in Nita City, as suffering from depression.

My friends, especially Professor Taylor, were very kind to me. Professor Taylor taught some of my classes. He also gave me an opportunity to vent about David and how badly he had behaved. I know I complained to him David lying to me about our relationship and about not getting the proper credit for my work at the Institute on the DOE grants. His advice was to get over it, get beyond my relationship with Simonson, and get on with my life. He also told me that it was unwise to attack Simonson personally or professionally and reminded me that Simonson could be vindictive. He told me that Simonson had broken off a relationship with a young woman member of the Public Policy faculty during Simonson's year as the dean of the school and that when she made some negative comments about him, the next thing anyone knew, she was gone from the University. I don't know her name or any of the details as I didn't get there until after she was gone, but I'm sure Professor Taylor does.

I tried to take Professor Taylor's advice, but I was still very angry and depressed and felt victimized. I'll admit that I did have some bad things to say about Simonson, both personally and professionally, to anyone who would listen both inside and outside the University including some of my public policy colleagues in other universities, but no one seemed surprised about what Simonson had done to me personally. Some people said that was his way and his history. As to the academic dishonesty of his taking credit for my work, no one seemed surprised by that, like it was a common occurrence for Simonson and others in academics.

I really had very little contact with Simonson that semester and I'll admit that I did not spend a lot of time at the Institute, and when I was there, I wasn't all that productive. I felt that if Simonson was taking credit for all the work on the projects that he should do some of it. It got back to me that David had some negative things to say about missed deadlines on the Department of Education project and Judith Harriman, who was the outgoing associate director of the Patterson Institute wrote me a memo (See Exhibit 8) and actually came to speak with me.

It was Judith's job at the Institute that had been offered to me as she had accepted an offer of a chaired professorship on the faculty of Conwell University where she was to become the director of the Wiseman Public Policy Institute. (Her position at Conwell University would have been similar to Simonson's at Nita University.) Judith talked with me about my work at the Institute. This was in early March YR-2. She told me it was time to straighten up and get back on track; that she was worried about me and my future at the University and the Institute. She also said that Simonson was not worth throwing away my career and that I had to meet the deadlines on my Institute projects. When I complained to her about Simonson taking credit for my work and my position that he should do what he was taking credit for she told me that attitude wasn't going to get me where I wanted to go and that it would be best if I just accepted the fact that I needed to be productive at the same level as I had before my break-up with Simonson. Judith then suggested I get some professional help. It was Judith who got me to Dr. Johnson.

After I started working with Dr. Johnson I seemed to get out of my funk and my classes certainly improved. I had missed the *American Public Policy Review*—or *APPR*—deadline, (See Exhibit 9) but was able to get some work done on that article and planned to get it out to publishers by that summer. As it turned out there was an opening in the

APPR Fall, YR-2 edition where the article was published. I also was able to catch up on most of my Institute work which included completing the report on the DOE grant due in July of YR-2 on public school privatization which was eventually re-funded. It was more difficult at the Institute that it could have been because Simonson was unavailable to me in person, partially because he was traveling a lot and partially, I believe, because he was embarrassed to meet with me face to face. Nonetheless, the work got done.

By the time May came around I was feeling much more like myself and was looking forward to getting tenure and moving into the associate director's job at the Institute. I had gotten the word from Judith Harriman in later April YR-2, that assuming everything went according to plan with tenure that Simonson had no objection to my taking on the associate director's job. In reality, the Associate Director is responsible for the day-to-day running of the Institute and there wasn't the need for a great deal of interaction with Simonson, whose job it was to promote the Institute and its work around the country and the world. I still had not had a one-on-one meeting with Simonson, but we had been in faculty and Institute meetings together and there were cordial but cool greetings and no obvious hostility. I was hopeful that we could keep the past in the past and go on with our professional relationship.

On May 5, YR-2 I got my tenure report (See Exhibit 10) from Professor Taylor who also serves as the chair of the tenurial faculty of the Public Policy School. It was a split, but positive report and I'll admit that the negative comments in the dissent were accurate regarding the missed publication deadline and the lower that usual class evaluations for the Spring YR-2 semester. In mid-May I got a call from Professor Taylor who asked me to come down to his office. When I got there, he was there with Professor Harriman.

Neither one of them looked very happy. Professor Taylor told me that there were some members of the public policy faculty who thought it would be better if I delayed my tenure vote for a year, as was suggested in the dissent in my tenure report. They said that in a year I could get out my article on public school privatization, regain my reputation as an excellent teacher, and perhaps be successful in obtaining some grant money for the University.

It was like they were talking through a fog. I was extremely upset. Professor Taylor said that he didn't personally agree; that he felt that I deserved tenure. Professor Harriman said her best advice was to wait a year, but that unfortunately, the associate director's position would have to be filled by someone else who was a tenured faculty member. I know that Professor Binder, who dissented on my tenure report was a disappointed candidate for the associate director's job and I felt that the whole thing was being rigged against me. Professor Harriman assured me that she did not believe that was the case, and told me that if I chose to go forward on the tenure vote and I was successful, that the Institute would stand by its offer, but she said that it was her best advice for the long term, that I wait a year and perform the way she knew I could and be assured of getting tenure. I told them I had to think about it and left in a daze.

I spent the afternoon with Dr. Johnson. I did most of the talking and in the end I decided that it was important to me to go forward that spring. First, I believed that I had earned tenure. My overall teaching and publications record was the equivalent of the faculty members in my peer group and the work I had done at the Institute had, in reality, brought grant money to the University. Professor Taylor had sent me a letter making the official offer to put over my tenure decision (See Exhibit 11). I told Professor Taylor of my decision to go forward in person and in writing (See Exhibit 12) and he said he would support me. I did get a call from Professor Harriman who tried to get me to change my mind. I asked her if Simonson was behind this and she said that she wasn't expressing any opinion other than her own but when I pressed her about Simonson, her reply was "What do you think? If you had both Professor Taylor's and Simonson's support, there wouldn't be a problem, would there?" I'm sure that Professor Harriman would confirm what she said to me, but as you probably know she died in a car crash in August YR-2 when driving in the mountains of Colorado.

After talking with Professor Harriman I called Professor Taylor back. He told me that he had done a head count and it looked like the vote of the faculty would be favorable and even though the dean of the Public Policy School had an independent vote, that neither Christine Jefferson nor any other Dean at the Public Policy School, had ever recommended against a faculty vote. I decided stick with my decision to go forward even though I realized that a negative vote or negative recommendation from Dean Jefferson would end my career at Nita University.

The tenure meeting was on June 1, YR-2. The only candidates were Bill Vasquez and myself. Professor Taylor told me that the faculty voted for tenure for both Bill and me, but that my vote was close, 15–12, with one abstention. I have since learned that it was Simonson who declined. Professor Taylor congratulated me and told me that I would hear from Dean Jefferson within a week or so. I was both relieved and frustrated; relieved about the positive vote and that I had apparently made the right decision, but frustrated that the vote was a lot closer than it should have been. Everything turned upside down the next week.

Dean Jefferson called me to her office the next week. She told me that it was a difficult decision, but that she had decided that it was not in the best interests of the University for her to recommend my tenure to the board of trustees; that she was sorry, but that her decision was final. I asked her what her reasoning was and she told me I would receive a letter from her. She told me the University was willing to keep me on the faculty for one semester and would assist in my finding a position with another University. At that point I lost it. I started to cry and yell at the same time. I told her she was wrong and that she should have had the courage to stand up to Simonson, that she was nothing more than a puppet. She cautioned me not to say anything that I would later regret; that my telling tales out of school had gotten me where I was and that I should be civil and take responsibility for my own actions, both personal and professional. I stormed out of her office and went home.

Three days later I received Dean Jefferson's letter. Exhibit 15 is that letter. It wasn't very specific, stating as the primary reason something about lack of collegiality on my part. It also mentioned the failure to publish the *American Public Policy Review* piece in the Spring, my lower than usual teacher evaluations and the failure to produce new grant money for the University through grants or otherwise. I of course do not agree with the letter or its conclusions and I wrote a short letter to Dean Jefferson stating as much. (See Exhibit 16).

For the next several weeks I spent my time trying to figure out what went wrong. I spoke with Professor Taylor several times and he was solicitous, but advised me to try to put everything behind me and work towards new goals. I also had daily sessions with Dr. Johnson, but despite her help I remained in a deep depression. Together we decided it would be good for me to make a clean break from the whole situation and I returned home. I did not stay on at Nita U through the Fall YR-2 semester as Dean Jefferson had offered, although I took a leave of absence without pay in order to be able to continue my health benefits. That leave was to end and did end on December 31, YR-2. I felt it would be awkward and unpleasant to remain on campus and have to face the people who rejected me on a daily basis. I was also still very angry at Dean Jefferson and Simonson. I believe that he was the prime mover against me with the dean. I did want to remain in academics although I realized it was too late to get anything for the Fall, YR-2 semester. I sold my condo, and even though I took a loss, selling it for $175,000, I cleared enough money to live on for the next period of time, so long as I lived with my parents.

While at home I continued my therapy with Dr. Ruth Steiner who was recommended to me by Dr. Johnson. By the end of July I was feeling considerably better, but no where near myself. I was depressed a lot. I didn't want to go out with my friends. I was uninterested in any contact with men or a social life of any kind. I missed teaching terribly and the interaction with my students and my colleagues. I felt as if my life had been stolen from me. I did improve little by little, but it wasn't until a year or so later when I was working again that I started to have what I would call a normal life.

During that same time period I met with a lawyer, Charles Twiggs, about my situation and he advised me that I had a possible claim against Nita University, Jefferson and Simonson for gender discrimination and other claims. I did what he advised and filed a claim with the Nita Equal Employment Opportunity Commission office (See Exhibit 17), as well as with the University of Nita (See Exhibit 18). I have never sued anyone in the past. I did complain to the University Committee on Discrimination once before in January or February YR-5 about some offensive conduct targeted at me by then Dean Dressler of the Business School that had been ongoing since the previous semester (See Exhibit 19).

During the Fall Semester of YR-6 I was assigned to a University Fund raising Committee as a representative, together with Professor Taylor, from the Public Policy School. Dean Richard Dressler was the chair of that committee. As part of that University service I attended a number of social functions. At each and every one of these functions, Dean Dressler would have a little too much to drink and he always ended up with his hands all over me, touching my shoulders, waist, and buttocks. Once he even brushed his hand over my breasts. He also made suggestions that I drive home with him or meet him privately. The first time it happened I made it clear I wasn't interested. If that had ended it, I would have never mentioned the matter again. When he persisted, including suggesting that I accompany him out of town on a fund raising trip, where we could get a suite together, I drew the line. I told Professor Taylor what had happened. He said that this was an old story with Dressler and that I should go to the University Committee on Discrimination. I took Professor Taylor's advice and made a confidential complaint to the committee. That was in January of YR-5.

I talked briefly with a Committee on Discrimination investigator and told her exactly what I just told you and never heard anything more from the University. I did get a call from Dressler. He was obviously drunk. He said that he hoped I was satisfied, that he was leaving Nita U and that I was responsible. I also got several anonymous notes Public Policy School letterhead blaming me for Dressler's leaving and saying what goes around comes around, things like that. I was upset by the notes but didn't do anything about them at the time. I didn't even tell Professor Taylor. I did keep the notes in a file (See Exhibits 20 and 21)

I now think that the whole Dressler episode had something to do with Dean Jefferson's decision. I'm told that she and Dressler were close and that she was upset when he left Nita U to become the president of Western State University in Conwell. I really don't think I had anything to do with his move but if Jefferson does, that might partially explain her coming down hard on me. I know that in my Yearly Review for YR-5 there was mention of lack of collegiality regarding my work on the University Fund raising Committee but I thought that had to do with my refusal (after Dressler's activity) to participate in committee social functions. I know that when I asked Dean Jefferson about her comment in the report, she wasn't specific, just saying that she was reporting generally what had been reported to her and that I should try to be more collegial.

I prepared a resume and submitted it to approximately a hundred universities. I got a couple of interviews, one at Nita State University and one at Columbus University of Conwell, in my home State, but no offers came from it. Given my resume, my publications record and my teaching record, I believed that I should have caught on somewhere. I heard from friends of mine at Nita State and Columbus that I was hurt in both places by getting letters from Simonson that were less than complimentary and from Dean Jefferson that damned me with faint praise. I got copies of those letters from a friend of mine at Columbus, Professor Jane Gianelli, who was on Columbus's hiring committee. (See Exhibits 22 and 23) I showed those letters to Professor Howard Gelson at Nita State and he told me that they were the same ones he had seen in my file at that institution. I should say that I never asked Simonson or Jefferson for letters on my behalf so their hurting my chances for another job was completely gratuitous. Even though Professor Taylor wrote me a great letter (See Exhibit 24), the overall picture from Nita U apparently did not merit my being hired by either Columbus or Nita State. Although

I have no specific information, I suspect that the same Simonson and Jefferson letters went to other institutions as well.

I discussed all of this with Mr. Twiggs and a legal complaint was filed originally in state court in Conwell where I was living at the time. I don't understand how it happened but eventually the case got transferred to the federal court in Nita City. I am not clear on all of the legal niceties but basically I believe that I was denied tenure because I ended my relationship with Simonson and that he, Jefferson, and the University retaliated against me by denying my tenure. I also know they caused me all kinds of emotional distress. Although I am better now, it has only been since the fall of YR-1 that I have been able to go out socially and actually have an enjoyable date with a man. I also miss my students and colleagues terribly and the intellectual interchange that was part and parcel of the University academic life. Simonson and Jefferson also hurt my employment chances with other universities through their denial of my tenure and the letters they sent out that were unfair and false or at least misleading in describing my qualifications.

As it turned out I ended up back in Nita City. Once I had struck out at the University level, I started to apply to some think tanks in Washington, D.C., New York, Boston, and Nita. In Spring YR-1 I got an interview with the Beecher Institute in Nita City. I was interviewed there by Dr. Rose Clemmons, Institute Director, and we hit it off both intellectually and on a personal level. I was frank with her about my troubles at Nita U and the fact that I was suing them. She told me that she needed to get a good recommendation from either Simonson or Jefferson as well as from Professor Taylor who had recommended me to her already. She said she knew Simonson and thought she could make things work.

I don't know what she did, but the letter she showed me from Simonson was accurate about my abilities and positive and I got the position as a senior researcher at the Beecher Institute. Exhibit 26 is that letter from Simonson. Dr. Clemmons told be that Simonson agreed to help me out and had told her that he wished me well at the Beecher Institute. I started on July 1, YR-1 and moved back to Nita City in June YR-1. I had used up most of what I had taken out of my house so I'm renting for now. Exhibit 27 is the offer letter I received from the Beecher Institute. My current salary from the Beecher Institute is $46,000 per year plus benefits that they calculate at 18 percent. The work is good, but opportunities for pay increase are relatively limited. Top earners at Beecher make about $60,000 a year, as compared to a full-tenured professor at Nita U where the average salary is $105,000. I also got a part-time teaching position at Nita Community College. It doesn't pay much, it will work out to about $7,500 per year for three evening courses each year, but at least I'm still teaching.

I really don't have any realistic hopes of ever landing a University teaching job in the future. I suppose I could get something with the a state government agency or perhaps at the federal level, but those jobs are limited to the political realties of changing administrations. I also have a personal reason for remaining in Nita City. I have recently (December 25, YR-1) become engaged to marry Thomas Fisher, who is a vice president with Nita Bank and Trust. We met in early October and he swept me off my feet. He's a great guy and as honest and forthcoming as a person can be. We plan to live and raise a family here in Nita City. It is my intention to continue to work. I enjoy the intellectual challenge of working. Although more solitary and not of the same kind or quality as the University, I am contented with my current job, not that I don't yearn for my past career. I might take family leave in addition to maternity leave from the Beecher Institute, but I will continue to work. It will not be as easy as if I was still with Nita University where they have great child care facilities, but my work is too important to me to leave it, even for children.

I have read this deposition and it is complete and accurate.

Mary Anne Williams

Mary Anne Williams

Subscribed and sworn before me this 29th day of March, YR-0

Margaret Moyer

Margaret Moyer
Certified Shorthand Reporter

This deposition was given under oath at the offices of the plaintiff's counsel on March 29, YR-0.

Deposition of David Simonson

My name is David Simonson. I am forty-six years old, married with two children, and live at 3600 University Drive in Nita City. I am employed by the University of Nita as the Patterson Professor of Public Policy in the Public Policy School and have the additional position of Director of the Patterson Institute for Public Policy. I was born and raised in West Hartford, Connecticut. I was graduated from the Choate Rosemary Hall Preparatory School in Wallingford, Connecticut and then attended and graduated from Harvard University summa cum laude with a bachelor's degree in Public Policy in YR-25. I was the only Harvard undergraduate student accepted that year into the Public Policy Ph.D. program and received my Ph.D. from Harvard in Public Policy in YR-21. By that time I had a number of publications, including several coauthored with my Harvard professors. I was heavily recruited by a number of universities and decided to accept an appointment as an Assistant Professor of Public Policy at Nita University.

Nita University was not the most prestigious University to make me an offer, but had a fine reputation in the area of Public Policy. I accepted the position primarily due to the fact that I had met my future wife, Kathryn Miller, who was then a resident at Massachusetts General Hospital and had accepted a position on the faculty of the Nita University's Franklin Medical College. Kathryn's family had a long association with Nita University, her father having served as the dean of the Medical School and her grandfather, as the president of the University. Kathryn's parents had been killed in a private plane crash and she wanted to move back home. Kathryn and I continued to date and were married in December of YR-21. We have lived ever since in her family home on University Drive. My daughter Debbie was born in YR-20 and my son, Steven in YR-18. I have had numerous opportunities to leave Nita University over the years but have always chosen to stay.

I have had a very successful career at Nita University and have been fortunate to be able to attract numerous grants from the government and private foundations to the Public Policy School over the years. I have also served on a number of government commissions and have acted as a consultant both to the White House and Congress over the years. I have consistently been evaluated as one of our top teachers and my publication record is unmatched by anyone else on our faculty. I am sure no one on the faculty would disagree with that statement. I was granted tenure and promotion to full professor in YR-16. Yes, that was significantly faster than the norm at Nita University. My early tenure and promotion was engineered by then-Dean Marvin Taylor of the Public Policy School, although it received unanimous support from my colleagues, and I am told, was easily approved through the central administration. I know the University was particularly pleased with the grant money that I had been able to attract, even as a junior faculty member.

In YR-9 I was appointed the Dean of the School of Public Policy. I replaced Professor Taylor as Dean. I wouldn't say it was an acrimonious process, although some of my supporters went overboard on my behalf, if not with my encouragement or knowledge. I understand that Professor Taylor's sexuality (he is gay) was the occasion for negative comment to some alumni and some people in the University administration. I did not and do not condone such activity and I am certain that Professor Taylor's private life was not a real issue in the decision-making process. Dean Taylor had always been very good to me. I just believed that it was in the best interests for the school and the University for there to be new leadership in the dean's office. At the time of my appointment Dean Taylor had been in his position for over fifteen years and it was just time for a change. At the time of my appointment I was still in my thirties and although that is young for such a position, I was the choice of both my colleagues and the central administration.

One of my first acts as Dean of the Public Policy School was to attract a significant contribution from the Patterson Foundation of $10 million. The contribution endowed the new Patterson Institute for Public Policy and the Patterson Chair in Public Policy. Gregory Patterson, Jr., President of the Patterson Foundation, is an old friend and although it took some cajoling and persuasion (as other universities were also courting him), he was very generous in his gift. Greg remains Chair of the Board of the Patterson Institute and was also appointed a university trustee. Unfortunately, Greg Patterson was insistent that I take on the position of the Director of the Patterson Institute, which he viewed as essential to the Institute achieving national prominence. I didn't feel that I could undertake that position and the deanship at the same time so I decided to resign as Dean of the Public Policy School. No, Greg Patterson did not insist on my resignation as dean. I was the one who felt the new Institute deserved by full attention.

My appointment to the directorship and as the Patterson Professor of Public Policy was announced in the spring of YR-8, at the same time as my resignation from the deanship. Professor Christine Jefferson of our faculty was named as my replacement as dean. You are correct that she was not the most distinguished of our teachers and scholars, but she was and is an excellent administrator and has done a fine job as our dean. Christine was the first female tenured professor in the Public Policy School and I was a strong supporter of her candidacy. It is also true that she was active in my candidacy for the deanship as I was, in turn, regarding her appointment as dean, and that we remain close colleagues, but her appointment had more to do with strong support she received from the Council of Deans, with then-Dean Dressler of the Business School leading the charge. I do not know the source of his admiration for Christine. I understand they are friendly, but that's all I know.

No, there was no other reason why I resigned as Dean of the Public Policy School. Yes, there was an allegation made to the University by Assistant Professor Lydia Greenfield of sexual harassment on my part at about the same time, but nothing ever came of it and she left the University on her own for a position with Nita State University that same year. It is true that Professor Greenfield and I had a sexual relationship that began shortly after she joined the faculty of the Public Policy School in the Fall of YR-9. When I was appointed the Dean of the Public Policy School as of January 1, YR-8, I felt it was inappropriate to be involved with a junior faculty member on whose tenure I would eventually have to make a recommendation, so I ended our affair. In truth, I believe the relationship was reaching an end anyway at that time.

I know that Professor Greenfield takes the position that she was the one who ended our relationship and that I continued to pursue her. That's not accurate. It is categorically false that I attempted to pressure her into continuing our relationship. If anything, it was the other way around. I also know that she filed a complaint against me with the University. I told University Counsel exactly what I have told you. I have no knowledge of how they worked it all out. As I said, I know that she left at the end of the academic year for a position at Nita State University where she has had a good, if unspectacular career. I am aware that Professor Taylor assisted her in obtaining that position. At the time that she made her complaint to the University, he (Professor Taylor) attempted to talk to me about the situation. Frankly, it was none of his business, so I put him off.

Professor Greenfield was not the first woman with whom I have had an extramarital sexual relationship, and I am answering your questions under protest. I really don't see why this is relevant to anything. My wife Kathryn is a committed cardiac thoracic surgeon who is married to her profession. She and I have both had extramarital affairs. We remain married as a matter of mutual convenience. We also believe it is best for us to stay together for the sake of our children. Kathryn and I share the same house. We do take family trips, vacations, and attend social functions within the University, and otherwise together, and over the years there have been periods of times, some of them extensive, when our sexual relationship has rekindled. But as I said, we have both had other sexual relationships. I know that this sounds odd, but it is the accommodation we have reached over the years. I doubt that we will ever divorce. I have never had any serious thoughts of doing so and to my knowledge, neither has she.

You are correct that I have had sexual relationships with other members of the University community over the years; not nearly as many as the rumor mill would have it. None of those relationships have been with undergraduate or graduate students. Such relationships are strictly forbidden by University policy. The relationships have always been consensual. They have always ended by mutual consent, although one of us would, as would be expected, tire of the relationship before the other. The relationships with Professor Greenfield and Professor Williams were the only ones with women in the Public Policy School. They are also the only two relationships where there have been formal complaints made to the University. Professor Williams is the only person with whom I have had a sexual relationship who has sued me and/or the University on the grounds of sexual harassment, discrimination, or otherwise. These allegations are completely without merit.

Yes, I do recall a professor from the business school named Janet Lane. I also recall a woman by the name of Doris Cocheran. She was the non-faculty administrator of the University's computer center. No, I did not have a sexual relationship with either of those two women.

I'll admit that I was attracted to Professor Lane. I met her many years ago, I believe it was in YR-15. She and I served on a University committee together and as a result we spent a good deal of time together. I thought that there was a mutual attraction and proposed to Professor Lane that we explore a more intimate relationship. I was persistent; many women want to be pursued. Apparently I was a mistaken or Professor Lane got cold feet, but for whatever reason she declined my advances and I dropped it. I wasn't happy about the rejection. Who ever is? But I wouldn't say I was angry and I certainly never threatened Professor Lane in any way, shape, manner, or form. Dean Taylor did talk to me about the situation and I told him what I told you. He was supportive as always. Dean Taylor knew about my less-than-perfect relationship with Kathryn. As a young faculty member he had talked to me about some rumors around the University about my having had an extramarital affair. I informed him about the nature of my relationship with Kathryn in general terms and assured him that I was not involved with any students. Quite appropriately, he dropped it at that. Professor Lane did leave the University for a position with the Department of the Treasury in Washington, D.C., but I had nothing to do with her leaving.

The situation with Ms. Cocheran was different. She was the director of the University's computer center and as such I had a good deal of interaction with her as we used the services of her department in performing statistical analyses of data collected pursuant to several grants I had obtained with the government for the University. It was Ms. Cocheran who was interested in me and I was the one who turned her down. Apparently she got upset and said something to the Chancellor about my pursuing her. Dean Taylor again spoke to me and I told him the reality of the situation. Ms. Cocheran and I did have some disagreements about the work her center did for me on my grants and the timeliness of their production of work product for me, but no, I never threatened her in any way. I am aware that Ms. Cocheran left the University sometime shortly after that, but that was certainly unrelated to anything involving me.

I readily admit my relationship with Professor Williams. I had visited her classes when she first joined the faculty (at her request) and was favorably impressed. When a position as a researcher came open at the Institute, I recruited her for the position. There were other applicants for the position, including Professor William Vasquez of our faculty. In my opinion, Professor Williams, who had actually one year less on the faculty than Professor Vasquez, was the far superior candidate. She did very good work for the Institute; her most significant contributions being on a series of grants from the U.S. Department of Education on public school privatization. She and I worked closely on those grants, and she drafted reports, most of which I adopted in very close to the form in which she drafted them. Yes, of course it was my name that went on those reports. I was the principal investigator on the grants and it is expected that the reports come from me. It is not unusual for a junior staff member such as Professor Williams to perform the drafting function without attribution. That is the way of the world in academic grant reporting. Professor Williams also prepared the applications for renewal of those DOE grants, which were successful. No, I don't believe that she was acknowledged in the application as the drafter of the application. I was the principal investigator and it was my contacts and reputation, not hers, that attracted the grant. Professor Williams was noted as staff on both the reports and the applications. That was her function on those grants.

It was during the work on the first report of that initial DOE grant that we became close and eventually began an intimate relationship. That would have been in the early summer of YR-4.

My personal relationship with Professor Williams lasted from approximately July YR-4 until January YR-2. We were well matched in temperament and interests. We spent a good deal of time together. I frequently visited her at her apartment, and later her condominium, and we would often attend professional meetings together. Our relationship was not a secret, although we did not go out of our way to publicize it. Kathryn knew of my relationship with Professor Williams. At the time she was in a relationship of her own with one of her colleagues from another medical school.

Professor Williams was a good junior colleague and as I said did fine work on the DOE grants at the Institute. She was also a competent member of the Public Policy School faculty. Her teaching was well received by the students and her scholarship well within the acceptable range. She had not yet attracted any new money to the University, but I believed at the time that she would be able to do so in the future. We had plans to submit grants applications together with Professor Williams listed as a principal investigator along with myself. In this way, I could ease her into the process and assist her in making a name for herself the public policy grants arena where I am well known and well regarded. Of course, as you know, that never happened.

My professional relationship with Professor Williams was a good one as well. Not only were we successful on the DOE grant, but I found her easy to work with and competent in dealing with staff and other professionals at the Institute. I was positive regarding her work in my oral reports to the faculty and my opinions and comments are reflected accurately in her YR-3 promotion letter that you just showed me (See Exhibit 6).

In Fall YR-3, Professor Judith Harriman, who was the associate director of the Institute announced that she would be leaving the University at the end of the academic year to accept a chaired professorship at Conwell University. Yes, I'm aware that unfortunately she died in a car crash in Colorado in the summer of YR-2. It was a real loss. At any rate, the associate director's job requires overseeing the day to day operation of the Institute. It is a position designed to allow me the time as the director to be the public face of the Institute and to seek public and private funding for our work.

It was decided that the position would be filled from inside the University. The job required that the associate director be a tenured member of the faculty and there were several candidates from the Public Policy School who already had tenure for the position. Professor Williams was one of two untenured junior faculty members, along with Professor Vasquez, who were also considered for the position. We also seriously considered Professor Binder of our faculty who was tenured at the time. After reviewing the applications and receiving advice from Professor Harriman I recommended that the offer of the associate directorship of the Institute be made to Professor Williams, conditioned upon her receiving tenure in YR-2. Exhibit 7 is my letter to Professor Williams offering her the associate director's position as of July 1, YR-2 and contains the condition that she be granted tenure.

It was anticipated at that time that Professor Williams would receive tenure, based on the facts of her performance as reflected in her promotion letter (Exhibit 6) including her work at the Institute on University grants, her teaching record and her scholarship which should have been enhanced by the planned publication of a major article arising out of the DOE grant on public school privatization in the American Public Policy Review in the spring of YR-2. You have shown me Exhibits 4A–4E. They were attached to Professor Williams's Tenure Report, which is when I first saw them, and I believe they accurately reflect her performance through YR-3. Of course, because Professor Williams did not receive tenure, she never fulfilled the conditions of that offer and the position was filled by Professor Binder of our faculty who has done an excellent job.

It is true that there is a connection of sorts between my personal relationship with Professor Williams and her eventual failure to receive tenure at the University, but that was really none of my doing. It was the actions of Professor Williams after our break up that eventually, as I understand it, persuaded Dean Jefferson that the tenure of Professor Williams was not in the best interests of the Public Policy School and the University. I will answer your questions about my relationship with Professor Williams but, as I've said, that relationship was certainly not directly related to her failure to receive tenure. Yes, I can explain that statement, and no it is not inconsistent with my previous testimony.

By the fall of YR-3 my personal and intimate relationship with Professor Williams had been ongoing for over a year. After her appointment as the next associate director of the Institute Professor Williams had purchased a new condominium and I did spend a good deal of time there and kept clothes and other personal items there, but whenever Kathryn was in town I always spent the night at home. It was never my intention to move into the condo and I don't know how there could have been a misunderstanding about that. I believed my relationship with Professor Williams to be a mutually satisfying one, with no commitments, but apparently she began to feel differently. In Fall YR-3, she began to make, at first veiled, and then explicit suggestions that I divorce Kathryn, so that I would be available for a permanent relationship with her. I probably could have been more direct, but I put Professor Williams off whenever she raised the topic. Yes, I probably said things like the time wasn't right or that the children were an impediment to a divorce (which was true), but the fact of the matter was that there was no chance of a divorce. No, I never told Professor Williams that Kathryn and I were in counseling prefatory to a divorce. I believe Professor Williams suggested counseling, but there never was any, and I never told Professor Williams that there was.

Over the holidays in YR-3, Kathryn and I and the kids went on a ski vacation as was our habit. During that vacation Kathryn and I reconnected, and Kathryn accompanied me to a conference in Europe in January. I had been to other conferences with Professor

Williams, but there was no plan for her to go along to that conference. Although Kathryn and I enjoyed each other's company, she made it clear that her relationship with another physician was ongoing and that she didn't want to end it. I intended to continue my relationship with Professor Williams, but on the same basis as before.

When I returned from the conference it was a hectic time what with the semester starting, but I eventually had dinner with Professor Williams at her condo. That would have been in late January. We had seen each other before that of course for only a few minutes at a time and usually in public. During that dinner, Professor Williams insisted that I divorce Kathryn and demanded an answer from me. I told her that wasn't going to happen. I may have said something about the children to let Professor Williams down easily, but no, I never said that they were in counseling about a divorce; as I said there wasn't any counseling.

Professor Williams's reaction was totally unexpected and totally out of line with our relationship. She became extremely angry. She called me every name in the book. I tried to just take it, she was obviously hurt and expecting or wanting more than I could give her. She felt that I had deceived her and called me a liar, among, as I said other things and I just took it, hoping that she would get over her anger. But when she accused me of academic dishonesty and of inappropriately taking credit for her work, I was unable to contain myself. I too became angry. I told her she was delusional; that she knew what our relationship was and what it wasn't. I also reminded her that I had been good for her professionally as well. No, I never threatened her in any way. Did I tell her to be careful of what she said, that I was her superior? Perhaps, a lot of things were said in anger. I just don't recall. I never intended to harm Professor Williams in any way. As I said, our relationship had been a good one. I assumed that her anger would subside, and I do admit that I hoped that we could resume our relationship, but even if we did not have a personal relationship there was no impediment, assuming civility, to continuing our professional relationship.

But Professor Williams seemed hell-bent on destroying herself. She made many accusations to our colleagues in the Public Policy School and apparently outside the University as well that I had lied to her about our relationship and more importantly that I was taking credit for her work and that she was the one responsible for the DOE grant success and its renewals. First, her accusations were wrong, and second, collegiality is an extremely valued characteristic within our school. I know that Professor Williams put off a number of my colleagues, and Dean Jefferson, as well, with her antics. How do I know this? There were conversations between myself and my colleagues, including Dean Jefferson. I tried to stay above the uproar. Given our relative positions and reputations I did now believe anyone was taking Professor Williams's rantings seriously. Unfortunately for her, I believe they left a sour taste in the mouths of many on the faculty. I also know that the comments about me, if not the source, got to Greg Patterson because he said something to me. I told him not to worry that there had been an academic disagreement and everything would blow over and be all right. He agreed to drop it, but said that he was concerned. No, I have never seen Exhibit 14 before. I was unaware that Greg had sent this to Christine Jefferson and I certainly did not ask him to do so. I can handle my own affairs. I don't need help from anyone.

As I understand it, Professor Williams's performance in the classroom also suffered as reflected in class evaluations. All of that is documented in her Tenure Report (Exhibit 10). I had nothing to do with the contents of that report in any way and saw it only when it was distributed before our tenure vote. I know that for a period of time she was a virtual no-show at the Institute, although she eventually completed all of her work and by the spring was performing again at an acceptable level. The Institute's offer to her to become the associate director was never withdrawn before the tenure decision. We had been civil to each other and the work was getting done and she was talented as an administrator. I was confident that she could do the job. Of course, when Professor Williams was denied tenure, the offer was withdrawn as she had failed to meet the contingency of the offer.

I did not vote on Professor Williams's tenure. I abstained. There was substantial opposition to her tenure. The reasons articulated at the meeting against tenure included her lower class evaluations for the Spring YR-2 term, her failure to attract new grant money to the University, and her failure to publish her planned article in the *American Public Policy Review*. I know that a suggestion had been made or at least the option given to Professor Williams that she put off the tenure vote for a year so that she could cure the perceived problems but she declined. Her supporters, headed by Professor Taylor, pointed to her complete history as a teacher arguing that the Spring YR-2 evaluations were a one-time lapse, her work on the DOE grant and its renewals and her acceptable publications history. No, I do not believe that any of the negative factors articulated would normally have been sufficient for a negative tenure vote. I believe that the real negative feeling on tenure was the result of her unprofessionalism in her attacks on me as evidence of lack of collegiality, and the concern that this behavior could be replicated in the future in other circumstances. I did not share that view in the meeting although I was concerned about potential future problems. Professor Williams's pettiness was cause for concern.

In the end, the faculty voted tenure by the barest of margins, 15–12 with my abstention. According to University regulations, the dean of the school has an independent recommendation regarding tenure that is required before tenure can be granted. Yes, the dean essentially has a veto. No, I know of no other instance in the Public Policy School when a dean has chosen to do so, but the authority of the dean exists for a reason. I know that Dean Jefferson agonized over her decision. She did ask me my opinion but I declined to say one way or the other what I would do. She asked if I was comfortable being on the same faculty with Professor Williams. I do not recall specifically what I said but no one likes to be called a liar and I may have said that, but, no, I never said I was uncomfortable being on the same faculty with Professor Williams. As I said, we had been civil in late Spring YR-2.

I did say to Dean Jefferson, what she already knew, that it was her duty to exercise her judgment and that I was sure that she would do the right thing for the Public Policy School, but I did not suggest how she should exercise that judgment. No, I did not point out that going against a faculty vote on tenure had never occurred at the school, but I'm sure she knew that. I do not know who else Dean Jefferson spoke with. It would have been appropriate to speak with Professor Taylor given his status as a senior chaired faculty member and as Chair of the Tenurial Faculty, but I don't know if she did so. It was her call, her decision and I'm sure she did what she thought was best for the school. I did not see Dean Jefferson's letter to Professor Williams before it was sent. Exhibit 15 is that letter. Dean Jefferson copied the letter to the tenurial faculty.

Because the semester was over and the faculty was dispersing for the summer, there was not an great outcry about Dean Jefferson's decision. There was some complaining in the fall, with Professor Taylor in the lead, but that was it. I know that Professor Williams was very upset. Of course, she would be. I think Professor Williams made a mistake by not staying on with the University for another semester which was offered to her by Dean Jefferson. It was in her letter. I know Professor Williams did apply for other faculty positions. I received numerous inquiries from other institutions as the Director of the Patterson Institute and yes I did compose a form letter to be sent to all of those Universities. Exhibit 23 is a copy of that letter. I believe it is a fair and accurate statement of Professor Williams's qualifications and her history at Nita University. No I never intended to harm her chances in any way. You have showed me a letter from Dean Jefferson regarding Professor Williams (Exhibit 22). I have never seen this letter before today. I agree the letters are similar, but after all we were talking about the same person and the same career.

I have heard rumors that Dean Jefferson may step down as dean and is considering a move to Western State-Conwell University where former-Dean Dressler of the Business School is the president. They have a long relationship. I did hear rumors years ago that they were romantically involved but, as I can attest to, there are a lot of rumors; some true, some false. I do not know what Dean Jefferson is going to do. She and I have not talked about her plans. I do know that Professor Taylor has made it uncomfortable for her. In addition, this lawsuit doesn't help with the alumni or the University, but I know of no actual tie between this lawsuit and her potential for making a move. Dean Jefferson has been in the job for a long time and it might be right for all concerned to make a change

I know that Professor Williams eventually caught on with the Beecher Institute in Nita City which is a political think tank run by Dr. Rose Clemmons. Rose is an old friend. She called in the spring of YR-1 and told me that she wanted to hire Dr. Williams and asked me for a recommendation to support her decision. I accommodated Dr. Clemmons. Exhibit 26 is that letter. It was written for its intended use and of course, the Beecher Institute is a private, non-academic entity with not the same concerns as a University. That is what explains the differences between Exhibits 23 and 26.

This whole incident has been an unfortunate one. I do not believe that what happened to Professor Williams was caused in any way by our relationship. This University has always been very good about separating the private lives of its faculty and staff members from their professional lives. Dean Jefferson exercised her best judgment as required by the University and she did what she thought was best. It was her job to make sure that the Public Policy School operates in an efficient and collegial way. I cannot criticize her decision. No, I will not speculate about what I would have done in this situation. It was not my judgment to make.

I have read this deposition and it is complete and accurate.

David Simonson

Subscribed and sworn before me this 12th day of March, YR-0

Harold Potts
Certified Shorthand Reporter

This deposition was given under oath at the offices of the plaintiff's counsel on March 12, YR-0.

Deposition of Christine Jefferson

My name is Christine Jefferson and I live at 1212 Harbor Center Court in Nita City, Nita. I am employed at the University of Nita as a Professor of Public Policy and the Dean of the Public Policy School. I am forty-eight years old and single. No, I have never been married. I am a graduate of Nita State University where I received my BA in Public Policy in YR-26. I received my Ph.D. in Public Policy from Conwell University in YR-21. I joined the Nita State University faculty as an assistant professor in the Public Policy School in that same year. In YR-18, I accepted a position, again at the assistant professor level at Nita University. I changed schools because of the better academic reputation of Nita University. I was promoted to associate professor in YR-15, and received tenure in that same year. I am aware that the vote was close, 12–10, but it was hard for women back then. I was the first woman to receive tenure in the Public Policy School. There are currently five women on the faculty of thirty-four professors; I am the only full professor, two others are tenured associate professors, and two young women assistant professors are untenured. I was promoted to full professor in YR-10. I have served as the Dean of the Public Policy School since YR-8. No, I would not consider myself the most distinguished member of the faculty of the Public Policy School. I am considered a good teacher and scholar by my colleagues. I feel my strengths are in administration.

My predecessor in the deanship was David Simonson who stepped down to become the Director of the Patterson Institute for Public Policy. He was also named the holder of the Patterson Chair in Public Policy at the same time. David had attracted the grant to fund the Chair and the Institute from the Patterson Foundation in that year and Gregory Patterson had insisted that he take on the Directorship of the Institute as a condition for making the gift to the University. David is now and has been for many years the acknowledged star of the Public Policy faculty. He is our best teacher, our best scholar, nationally well-regarded, the member of numerous government commissions, a consultant to state, local, and national government entities and the source of many, many grants to the University.

I believe that Mr. Patterson's insistence is the only reason for David stepping down as dean. Yes, there were rumors about David and the University being sued by a young woman assistant professor on the Public Policy faculty named Lydia Greenfield, but I do not know their accuracy. I do recall that David and Lydia were an item right before he became Dean and David has since told me that he ended that relationship when he became Dean and that Lydia was quite upset. But that's all hearsay and really none of my business. I do know Lydia left the University for a similar position at Nita State University where she is well-regarded. I have no reason to believe that the situation with Lydia Greenfield had anything to do with David stepping down as the dean and have no information about whether there was any legal action contemplated or begun regarding the situation.

No, that was not the first time I had heard rumors about David Simonson. According to the grapevine, he was in a very unhappy marriage, and although he and his wife remained together, it was at best, an unusual marriage where both parties felt free to explore romantic relationships outside the marriage. To each their own, I always say. I know that when I joined the faculty that the rumors about David already existed. No, he never made an advance towards me. Yes, I've heard about other relationships he's had.

Yes, I do recall a situation many years ago, I'd say fifteen years or so ago where there was a misunderstanding between David and a woman on the Business School faculty. I believe her last name was Lane. Then-Dean Richard Dressler of the Business School, is an old and dear friend of mine and he mentioned at the time that David had been a little aggressive in pursuing a Professor Lane and that she had complained to Richard. Richard, in turn, spoke to the Dean Marvin Taylor at the Public Policy School and I believe everything was handled informally. It's true that Professor Lane left the University shortly thereafter, but I believe she took a government position. Richard, Dean Dressler, never told me that there was a cause and effect relationship between David's actions and her leaving, but you're right he never said there wasn't either.

Yes, I'm aware that Richard Dressler is the current President of Western State University in Conwell, our neighboring state. As I said Richard is an old and dear friend. Yes, I am aware that Professor Mary Anne Williams complained about Richard several years ago to the University Committee on Discrimination. Yes, she's also the plaintiff in this case; they are one in the same person. That was about five years ago, right before Richard left to become Western State-Conwell University President. Williams claimed that Richard had made improper advances towards her and had touched her in an inappropriate way. I believe she made more of the circumstance than it warranted. They were both single at the time and I believe the activity she complained of occurred in a social event or a number of social events involved in University fund raising while the two served on the same University committee where alcohol was served. Richard gets a little amorous when he drinks. No, we have never been romantically involved. We are friends. Richard confided in me that he was very upset by the whole thing. Do I think that Williams's accusation contributed to Richard Dressler leaving the University? I'm sure it didn't help, but I know that he had aspired to becoming the President of a University and he is very happy at Western State. No, I have never seen Exhibits 20 and 21 before. Of course they weren't written by me or anyone I know and I resent your accusation.

No, I do not believe that the University is overly permissive regarding sexual relations between members of the University community. There is a strict no-tolerance policy regarding sexual relations between faculty members and students of any kind, either undergraduate or graduate and that is appropriate. Faculty members are, and should be, free to associate with whomever they want. I agree that it is probably a bad idea for a dean to have a relationship with a person on their faculty because of potential appearance problems in course assignments, resource allocation, raises and tenure recommendations. But that is left to the sound judgment of the dean and faculty member involved. I'm sure that's why David Simonson ended his relationship with Lydia Greenfield when he became the dean. No, I personally would never have am intimate relationship with a member of my faculty while I am the dean. For me, that would be contrary to my personal sense of ethics with too many potential problems, but adults should be allowed to make adult decisions without interference from the University. If someone oversteps their bounds, there is a University Committee on Discrimination and other legal recourse available.

I'll agree that the relationship between David and Professor Williams presented some difficulties when it ended, especially given her status as a researcher at the Institute, but that was because of Professor Williams's inability to separate the professional from the personal. I don't believe policy should be made to cover the odd, unusual or unexpected situation or in anticipation of immature and unprofessional actions and reactions such as those exhibited by Professor Williams.

Yes, I'll be happy to discuss the merits of my decision not to recommend Professor Williams for tenure to the University. Professor Williams had a very good career at Nita University but that does not, and should not guarantee tenure. You are correct that Exhibits 4A–4E are my yearly reports to Professor Williams regarding her performance and I believe they are accurate. But you must remember, tenure is a lifetime commitment by the University to a faculty member and the decision is one that needs to be carefully made. Exhibit 1 is a copy of our standards for tenure and promotion. They require that for a faculty member to be granted tenure at the Associate Professor's level that the faculty member must show evidence of outstanding performance in two of three categories; scholarship, teaching and service. Contained within the service requirement in the Public Policy School, in this day and age is the demonstrated ability to attract outside funding in the form of grants to the University.

As Professor Williams's tenure report shows (See Exhibit 10) the three person review panel, in a divided vote, concluded that Professor Williams was an outstanding scholar and teacher and had demonstrated excellence in service to the Public Policy School and the University by her service on School and University Committees and through her work on a Department of Education grant on Privatization of Public Schools that had been made to the University through the efforts of David Simonson and renewed several times with significant input from her. The dissenting faculty member expressed concern regarding all three categories. He noted that Professor Williams had missed a deadline for an important article on school privatization scheduled for the Spring Issue of the *American Public Policy Review*, that her class evaluations for the Spring YR-2 semester were down from previous reviews, and that although she had done good work on the DOE grant (Yes, I did receive Exhibit 5D from David Simonson that reflects that work), she had not yet attracted any grants to the School on her own.

In light of the non-unanimous nature of the report, I know that Professor Taylor, the Chair of the Tenurial Faculty, gave Professor Williams the option of putting her tenure decision over for a year, but she declined. Exhibits 11 and 12 reflect that activity although I had nothing to do with that offer and Professor Williams's decision. I do believe, however, that she might have benefited from putting her tenure vote over, but that is really speculative.

The tenure report reflected the view of the tenurial faculty in general. The discussion was roughly along the lines of the report and in the end the tenurial faculty voted for tenure by a vote of 15–12 with one abstention by David Simonson. The closeness of the vote was significant to me and I believe reflected some disquiet on the part of the tenurial faculty regarding Professor Williams's collegiality and professionalism. It was then for me to perform my independent function regarding tenure by either supporting the vote of the tenurial faculty or by vetoing the tenure recommendation. I will agree that going against a vote of the tenurial faculty is extremely unusual in the University and to my knowledge had never occurred in the Public Policy School.

Nonetheless, after agonizing over the decision I determined that it was not in the long-term interests of the Public Policy School and the University for Professor Williams to receive tenure. The basis for my decision is set out in my letter to Professor Williams (See Exhibit 15).

One of the most important aspects in the efficient and effective performance of any school in the University, and in particular, in smaller faculties such as the Public Policy Faculty where we have twenty-nine tenured faculty members with the addition in YR-2 of Professor Vasquez, and five untenured faculty members, is collegiality. We must work together as a faculty on a daily basis, and at a minimum we must treat each other with respect and civility, even when we disagree.

Unfortunately, in the early winter of YR-2, Professor Williams took it upon herself to attack and disparage a senior and distinguished member of the Public Policy School, claiming essentially that he had plagiarized her work and the he was academically and personally dishonest. Yes, of course I am talking about her attacks on David Simonson. Professor Williams's comments made within, and outside, the University community were persistent for several months and had the potential of harming us within the world of academics and further, in our ability to attract soft money to the University. I had even received a letter from Gregory Patterson, Jr., Chair of the Board of the Patterson Foundation and a member of the University Board of Trustees, expressing some concern about comments attributed to a junior member of our faculty regarding David Simonson that had gotten to him through the grapevine, and their potential negative effect in world of charitable foundations (See Exhibit 14). Of course his letter is non-specific to Professor Williams, and based on rumors, but image is everything when trying to attract soft money and although Patterson's letter did not make my decision, it did make my decision easier. The letter confirmed my fears about the potential impact of Professor Williams's behavior and whether lifetime job security with the University was in the interests of the School and the University.

So in the end it was my judgment that Professor Williams had not demonstrated the kind of collegiality that is essential to the effective and academically prosperous operation of an academic institution. As a result, but with great sadness and disappointment I determined not to recommend her for tenure. My decision was final and had the effect of vetoing her tenure at the University. I offered her the opportunity to stay on for another semester

(See Exhibit 15) while she looked for other employment opportunities in academia and otherwise, but she declined and took an unpaid leave of absence for the Fall 2002 Semester after which her employment with Nita University was terminated.

I don't like to speculate, but absent the factors I have listed above, I suppose that Professor Williams's record would have warranted a position tenure recommendation on my part. Her qualifications were roughly equivalent to those of Professor Vasquez who was voted tenure by a near unanimous vote. As his report states, he was rated as outstanding in the areas of scholarship and service and excellent in teaching. (See Exhibit 13) It is true that the DOE grant on which Professor Williams worked generated more money for the University ($450,000 per year for the life of the grant which is ongoing) than Professor Vasquez (approximately $150,000 per year for the past several years). The DOE grant was and is, however, a David Simonson grant, even though Professor Williams made significant contributions to its success, and the Professor Vasquez grants were generated by him in his own name.

I have told you the entire basis for my decision regarding Professor Williams's tenure. No, David Simonson did not lobby me in a negative way regarding Professor Williams's tenure. I sought his counsel, after all he was the target of her attacks, and he declined to comment saying he was too close to the situation to be objective. I specifically asked him is he was comfortable being on the same faculty with Professor Williams and although he did not like her comments about him (who would), he confirmed his earlier statement that the decision was mine and should not be based on his feelings. I should be clear that this decision was not a Simonson versus Williams situation. Despite the nature of her comments about him David remained a gentleman and above the fray. I know that he even stood by the offer of the Patterson Institute to make Professor Williams its associate director, conditioned, as it was, on her receiving tenure.

Is David Simonson an important member of our faculty? Of course he is. He is the source of enormous prestige and important funding to the University and the School. Of course, his value to the University was greater than that of Professor Williams, that too goes without saying, but if your implication is I did not recommend tenure for Professor Williams to please Simonson, Patterson, or anyone else you are way off base. I have stated my reasons and stand by them.

No, Professor Williams claims regarding Richard Dressler had nothing to do with my decision. She was entitled to make whatever claim she thought appropriate to the University Committee on Discrimination and it would be inappropriate for me to even consider such activity and I did not. I do recall getting some complaints about Professor Williams' collegiality on the University Fund Raising Committee in YR-5, but they were non-specific and unrelated to any claim she may have made about Richard. As I've said several times, I have told you the basis for my decision and there was nothing else involved. No, I did not view the Patterson letter as suggesting that I not recommend Professor Williams's tenure. It did however, as I said, confirm my fears regarding the potential damage her behavior could have to the Public Policy School.

I did receive inquiries from a number of universities to which Professor Williams applied for faculty positions. I did write letters to them at their request and I believe that those letters, which were all identical in substance, were accurate regarding Professor Williams and her qualifications. Exhibit 22 is a copy of my letter. I do not view my letter as negative. Nor do I view it as a glowing recommendation. As I said, I believe it to be fair and accurate. I have never seen David Simonson's letters regarding Professor Williams (Exhibits 23 and 26) before today. I had nothing to do with either letter.

My decision regarding Professor Williams's tenure has not been without ramifications. Professor Taylor has been particularly outspoken in criticizing my decision both within the University and with our alumni. Many of my colleagues are also upset about my decision. Many of my colleagues have also supported my decision. As I said it was a difficult one. Do I think that I can be effective as the Dean of Public Policy School? That remains to be seen, but if I don't think I can be a good leader for our school I will step down. I do not want to do so or to leave the University but those options are available. Nita City and the University are home to me. I have had no formal discussions with anyone regarding either stepping down as dean or a position with another university. Yes, Richard Dressler has tried to recruit me to join the Western State-Conwell University but those conversations have been on-going on an informal basis for years, way before this entire incident. No, I do not hold Professor Williams responsible for any difficulties I have had in the School or University. I am a professional and I made a professional decision and I remain convinced that I did the right and correct thing and I am more than willing to live with my decision.

I have read this deposition and it is complete and accurate.

Christine Jefferson

Christine Jefferson

Subscribed and sworn before me this 29th day of March, YR-0

Margaret Moyer

Margaret Moyer

Certified Shorthand Reporter

This deposition was given under oath at the offices of the plaintiff's counsel on March 29, YR-0.

DEPOSITION OF MARVIN TAYLOR

My name is Marvin Taylor and I live at 3501 University Drive in Nita City, Nita. I am sixty-six years old and live in a monogamous relationship with Howard McDonald, who is the retired Headmaster of Nita Academy, a private prep school here in Nita City. We have been together for twenty years. I am the John and Mary Beecher Professor of Public Policy at Nita University. I have held that chair for twenty-five years. I also serve as the Chair of the Tenurial Faculty at the Public Policy School. I am a graduate of Nita University and obtained my Ph.D. in Public Policy from Conwell University in YR-40. That very same year I was hired on to the faculty of the Public Policy School of Nita University and I was promoted through the ranks until I received tenure as a full professor in YR-33. From YR-25 through YR-9 I served as the Dean of the School of Public Policy.

It's true that I was replaced as Dean of the Public Policy School by Professor David Simonson. Of course he did what he could to obtain the position and there were faculty politics involved that can get a little nasty and did in this case. This was essentially a changing of the leadership guard event in the Public Policy School with David leading the young guard. It's also true that some of David's supporters made pejorative comments about my sexuality. Frankly, I have been gay all of my life and openly so for over twenty years. I am used to such behavior by uninformed people and expect that it will occur. Fortunately, things have been changing for the better and of that I am pleased. I do not believe that David Simonson was behind these attacks. I do not hold him responsible for them either, although I suppose I would have expected that he could have kept his supporters on the legitimate academic issues involved. But that's not always possible. No, he did not so-called "out" me. I was already "out" and had been for many years.

I will say that once David became dean he treated me with the respect and deference that I believe I had earned. When David resigned the deanship one year later in YR-8, I was approached to resume my position as dean, but declined because I believed it was time for the younger generation to takeover. One of David's group, although certainly not the most talented, Professor Christine Jefferson, became the dean and has done a reasonably good job given her abilities and reputation as a scholar, until, of course, this mess with Mary Anne Williams. I believe that in this matter Dean Jefferson has thwarted the will of the faculty and used her position in an inappropriate way.

I believe that Professor Williams being denied tenure by Dean Jefferson is bad policy and bad for the University and the Public Policy School. It has opened old wounds and I am afraid that her time as dean must come to an end for the good of this academic institution. In fact, were it not for Professor Williams's law suit against the University I suspect that she would already be replaced. I have it on good information that Jefferson is discussing a position with her old friend, Richard Dressler, former Dean of our Business School, and the current President of Western State-Conwell University in our neighboring state of Conwell. Dressler was a supporter of Jefferson's within the Council of Deans of the University and instrumental in her replacing David Simonson as the Dean of the Public Policy School in YR-8. As I said, there were other, more qualified younger faculty members who would have been better choices, but Dressler and Simonson prevailed upon the President of the University to appoint Jefferson.

I do not know the source of the Dressler/Jefferson alliance. I have been told that their relationship was a personal one, but that is none of my concern. My opinion of her ability is based on her teaching and scholarly performance as evidenced by her rather ordinary record of teaching and scholarship before her appointment as Dean. What's ironic is that Jefferson was voted tenure by the Public Policy School faculty in YR-15, by the barest of majorities, I recall the vote as being 12–10 in her favor. It's true that she was the first woman to receive tenure in the Public Policy School but I do not believe that had anything to do with the closeness of the vote. In fact, her gender may have been a benefit. The vote was a reflection of the problems in her performance as a teacher and a scholar. And even though as the dean I was entitled to an independent vote according to our regulations (See Exhibit 1) that could act as a veto of the faculty will, and even though I did not personally believe her candidacy to have merit, I did what I thought was best for the school and recommended her tenure to the University. As evidence of Jefferson's mediocrity, she was not promoted to full professor at the time of tenure which was the custom back then. "Full professor" rank is more difficult to attain these days and many faculty members in the University spend their entire careers after tenure at the Associate Professor level. Jefferson's promotion did not occur until YR-10, five years later, which, as I said, was unusual back then.

It is true that David Simonson was a supporter of Jefferson's for both tenure and later the Deanship. I truly believe that he saw Jefferson as a sure supporter of his agenda within the School and championed her tenure because of it. I also believe that David supported her deanship so that he could have some control of the Public Policy School even after he lost his deanship. It is well known that David has Jefferson's ear in all matters and is very influential with her.

Yes, I did say that David lost his deanship. I know that the official University line is that David left the deanship to assume the directorship of the newly formed Patterson Institute. That position, director, is essentially one designed to foster and promote the Institute and to assist in obtaining grants from the government and private foundations. That job could have been performed just as easily out of the dean's office and David could have easily held both positions. At the Institute, David, quite appropriately, has served as the public face of the Institute. The day to day operation is handled on the business/personnel level by an Administrator and at the policy academic level by the assistant director, with input from David at the top-end. David could easily have performed those functions he now performs as the Patterson Institute Director and remained the dean of the School.

I am relatively confident that David lost his deanship because he insisted on mixing his personal life with his professional life. Apparently, and David has said this to me himself, his marriage to his wife Kathryn, who is a well-respected surgeon, is not a good one.

David, on more than one occasion, has said to me and others than he only has stayed in the marriage for the sake of his children. It is well-known within the Public Policy School and the University generally that David has had numerous extramarital affairs with junior faculty members over the years. He has not been very discreet in that regard. There are also rumors that he has been involved sexually with undergraduate and graduate students, but that would be contrary to strict University policy and would result in termination from the University. I do not believe that David would ever have been that reckless.

Sexual relationships between consenting adult faculty members are not prohibited by the University and shouldn't be. Of course there are dangers in such relationships but absent the student-faculty fiduciary relationship, the University should not be concerned with the private sexual lives of its faculty members. This issue has been debated many times and in many forms over the years and fortunately, to date, the University takes the position that although sexual relationships between junior and more senior faculty members are not encouraged because of potential dangers of improper influence, favoritism and the like, that neither are they banned by University policy. Redress for inappropriate use of faculty power is left to the University Committee on Discrimination and lawsuits like this one, that are actually rare in our community.

I do know of three particular sexual relationships that David Simonson had with women faculty members over the years before his relationship with Professor Williams, all of which ended badly for the women involved and the University as well. By way of background, David Simonson came to us in YR-21 after a distinguished record at Harvard University where he received his Ph.D. In that same year. He already had several very well regarded publications and his teaching evaluations as a graduate assistant were extraordinary. At Nita University his academic performance in terms of teaching and scholarship was superb, and his University service exemplary, including within several years on the faculty he beginning to attract and obtain grants from both the government and private foundations to support his research and the research of several of his colleagues. Those grants also supported numerous graduate students and their research. Frankly I thought that we would lose him to a more prestigious University, but with his marriage to Kathryn (who is from an old and respected family in Nita City, her father was the Dean of the Medical School and her grandfather served as University President many years ago, even before my time) and her ties to the University's Franklin Hospital and Medical School, together with our fast tracking him through tenure and promotion, we were able to secure his services. As an academic David's reputation is unblemished. He is, with all deference to my colleagues, the star of our faculty. Oh yes, he is certainly better regarded in the national academy and otherwise than I am. I had my day, but when I say he is the star of our faculty, that is without qualification or exception. Perhaps that's why the University turns a deaf ear to his inappropriate predatory activities.

His inability to separate his profession from his personal life I believe could be considered David's Achilles heal. His reputation is of a sexual predator and I suppose his intellectual power has been found compelling, because by all reports, relationships within both the Public Policy Faculty and within the University as well have been common over the years. The rumors began within a year of his joining the faculty, I'd say beginning in YR-15 was the first I heard. I discounted the rumors because David appeared to be happily married and about that time his daughter was born and shortly thereafter his son. As a courtesy to David, who was untenured at the time, I raised the topic of these rumors in a private conversation. I don't recall the date but it was probably in YR-19. He denied any involvement with students, undergraduate or graduate, and I believed him. He did say that he and Kathryn were going through a rough spot after the birth of his daughter, but that he hoped and believed that everything would work out for their marriage. Although he did not admit infidelity, and I did not ask him to (absent a violation of University policy it was none of my business), he did not deny extramarital relations with members of the University community other than with students of any kind. My only comment was for him to take care as I was in the process of trying to engineer an early tenure and eventual early promotion to full professor for him with the University.

In the Fall of YR-15, I was approached by then Dean Richard Dressler of the Business School about an allegation by a young, untenured assistant professor on his faculty, Professor Janet Lane, that David had made improper advances towards her. I recall this specifically because Dressler was an unlikely source for such a complaint given his own reputation for such activity. Nonetheless, at Dean Dressler's request I spoke to Professor Lane who repeated the allegation. She said that David had approached her while the two served on a University committee and proposed, in explicit terms, that the two begin a sexual affair. Apparently David was quite persistent and in an apparent effort to persuade her, had said that he had a lot of influence in the University and that he could be very helpful to Professor Lane's career. According to Professor Lane, when she declined his advances David became rather angry and told her that she would regret her decision. Because Professor Lane felt vulnerable she went to Dean Dressler who, according to both her and Dressler, assured her that she had nothing to worry about. It is true that David had been granted early tenure and full promotion that previous spring in YR-16 and also that he had some cachet within the University because of the grant money he attracted, but he certainly had no influence in the Business School of which I was aware. I gave Professor Lane similar assurances to those given by Dean Dressler and told her I would speak to David, which I did.

When I spoke with David about Professor Lane's concerns, he began by saying that he and his wife Kathryn were having another difficult stretch and that they were considering a separation. He confided in me that not only he, but Kathryn as well, had been unfaithful. He admitted that he was attracted to Professor Lane and that he had felt that the attraction was mutual. He further stated that he proposed a liaison with Professor Lane and that she had declined. He denied suggesting he could be helpful to her career or threatening her in any way. He did say that her rejection bruised his ego and that he was less than happy about the situation. I advised him to stay away from Professor Lane. I also told him I was sorry to hear about him and Kathryn, especially because I knew that they had two small children. He thanked me for my concern. I believed that was the end of the matter, but I learned from Dean Dressler at the end of that semester in December of YR-15, that according to Professor Lane, David had persisted in his advances towards her, and that she had decided to leave the University and accept a position with the Department of the Treasury as a result. Professor Lane, according to Dressler and by reputation, was an excellent faculty member, and I called her to try to persuade her to stay at the University. She was polite, but told me her mind was made up and that she was leaving.

Although there were persistent rumors about David, the next incident of which I became specifically aware occurred in YR-11. This time it involved David and a woman named Doris Cocheran, who was a non-faculty administrator of the University computer center. Ms. Cocheran had complained to the University Chancellor that David, who used the services of the Computer Center in compiling statistics and statistical analyses on various studies conducted pursuant to grants he solicited on behalf of the University, had made improper sexual advances to her. According to the Chancellor, Ms. Cocheran stated that David had suggested a sexual relationship with her and that when she declined he "warned" her that his grants helped pay the freight for the Computer Center and her job. The Chancellor asked me to speak with both Ms. Cocheran and David. Ms. Cocheran who told me the same thing she had told the Chancellor and that she felt intimidated by David. When I spoke with David he denied any advances towards Ms. Cocheran. He did say that he interacted with her on his various grants but that was it from his point of view. He did say that Ms. Cocheran had flirted with him and even though he and Kathryn, again according to him, were married only in name and only for the children, that there were "a lot of fish in the sea" and that he told Ms. Cocheran in clear terms that he wasn't interested. I asked if he had ever threatened Ms. Cocheran in any way, and while he denied any threats he did say that he had reminded her that his grants helped pay for the computer center when he didn't believe he was getting prompt service from the center.

I reported the conversation with David to the Chancellor. I was informed by her that whatever occurred, that Ms. Cocheran had resigned her position with the University to take a similar position, for more pay, with the Nita Fire and Casualty Company.

The most serious problem with David and his sexual activities occurred, as I alluded to earlier, after he became the Dean of the Public Policy School in YR-9. Apparently, David and Lydia Greenfeld, who at the time was a first-year assistant professor in the Public Policy School, had a brief sexual relationship beginning before David became dean in the fall of YR-9 and continued for a month after his deanship began in January of YR-8. I was made aware of this fact by Professor Greenfeld who I had mentored regarding her teaching and scholarship. In late January of YR-8 she came to my office in tears. She related to me that shortly after her joining the faculty in the fall of YR-9, David started flirting with her, and that one thing led to another and they eventually began a sexual relationship. She said that she consented to the relationship, but that David had been the aggressor and that she had felt overwhelmed by him. She said that the relationship was particularly unsatisfying to her because David made her to feel subservient to him, and frequently made it clear to her that he was the star of the Public Policy Faculty and that she was just starting out. According to Professor Greenfeld, she eventually tired of the relationship and decided to end it. She said that she was particularly uncomfortable with David being named to the deanship of the Public Policy School with ultimate authority over her career.

Again, according to Professor Greenfeld, when she told David of her decision to end the relationship in December of YR-9, he became cold and threatening and told her that it was unwise for a person in her position to get on his bad side and insisted that the relationship continue. She told me that she had been worried about David's reaction so she had hidden a tape recorder in her purse which was on the night stand next to her bed in her apartment where the conversation took place. She played the recording to me and although David didn't sound threatening to me he did say in words or substance that Professor Greenfeld was in a vulnerable position. I can't remember the exact words but that was the clear import of what he said. She told me that she was extremely upset, that she was going to contact a lawyer, but that her real goal was to get out of Nita University with her reputation intact and on to another public policy school faculty. I tried to persuade her to hold off on the lawyer but she made no promises. I did tell her that I was sure I could help obtain another faculty position although I tried to persuade her to stay but to no avail. She was quite talented in my opinion.

I called David and tried to talk to him about the situation. I had just about gotten the subject of my call out of my mouth when he abruptly told me that he had to get off the phone. When I suggested that we meet in person he told me that it wouldn't be necessary, that he would handle the situation.

My next involvement with the situation was when I was contacted by University Counsel. I was told not to reveal the contents of that phone call and my later discussions with him and I will not do so. What happened to Professor Greenfeld? I can say that I was able to help place her on the Public Policy School faculty at Nita State University where she has prospered. She is a well-respected tenured Full Professor there and I have had the pleasure of reading her many fine articles and have appeared on panels with her. She is quite excellent in her profession; it was a real loss for us when she left. Yes, she did tell me before she left the University after the Spring YR-8 term, that the University paid her some money, although she said she couldn't say how much because of an agreement she had. In addition, she told me that she didn't believe that David would be dean much longer but couldn't say why. No, I do not have a copy of the tape she played for me. According to Professor Greenfeld all copies have been destroyed

As it turned out, Professor Greenfeld was correct. In June YR-8 David resigned as Dean of the School. At the same time he was named the Patterson Professor of Public Policy and Director of the newly formed Patterson Institute for Public Policy. It is well known that David was instrumental in attracting the Patterson Foundation money to the University that funded his chair and the Institute. Gregory Patterson, Jr. is his friend, and also an influential member of the University Board of Trustees. I am confident that his resignation was part and parcel of what he did to Professor Greenfeld and being named to the Institute position was a face saving move on the part of the University, but you would have to talk to David, the University lawyers or Professor Greenfeld to find out the answer for sure.

I met Mary Anne Williams during the interviewing process in the early part of the Spring Semester YR-8. I was part of the recruiting committee for the school and took an instant liking to her. She was being recruited by a number of Universities, given her record at the Sanford School at Duke, and her excellent interviewing skills. I know that David, too, was impressed with her and recruited her heavily to join our school. Her appointment as an Assistant Professor in the Public Policy School was approved in May YR-8 by the University and she accepted our offer and began to teach on our faculty in the Fall YR-8 Semester.

Despite our age difference, Professor Williams and I formed an instant good working and personal relationship. I was able to assist her in her teaching, suggesting successful methods I had used and observed, advised her on writing projects and helped in getting them published and generally was available to give her career advice. Exhibits 4A–4E, which you have showed me, chronicle her career at the school quite well. I have assisted many young people over the years, even David Simonson although I'm sure he wouldn't acknowledge the fact given his ego. Professor Williams also became a friend and from time to time would come to our home for dinner and other gatherings. She was a delightful addition to our circle of friends and Howard and I became quite fond of her.

It is true that I advised Professor Williams that an association with the Patterson Institute and with David Simonson would be helpful to her career. She needed to develop the ability to write grant applications and attract money to the University in order to be successful in a modern career as a public policy academic. The need to attract money to the University is an economic and academic fact in today's world and is even mentioned in our tenure guidelines under the rubric of University service, something you never would have seen thirty years ago. Exhibit 1 is a copy of those tenure guidelines. David Simonson, in addition to his academic brilliance and national reputation was the master of successful grantsmanship. It was my opinion, and I told Professor Williams directly, that she could benefit in many ways from a professional relationship with David so when she was given an opportunity in YR-6 to work with him as a researcher at the Institute, I advised her to do so and she accepted that position.

I did have some trepidation about David and his sexual aggression as evidenced in the situations with Professor Lane, Ms. Cocheran, and Professor Greenfeld, and then there were numerous other rumored affairs and so I told Professor Williams to be careful. She assured me that she was aware of David's reputation and that she could take care of herself. And Professor Williams seemed to prosper at the Institute. By all reports she was doing excellent for them, particularly in the area of privatization of public schools which became a scholarly interest for Professor Williams. The work at the Institute was broadening her horizons and it was well known that she was responsible for doing a lot of the work on a significant Department of Education grant regarding privatization of public schools, had written excellent reports on the grant, and in fact, according to David's reports to the tenured faculty of the school, had been responsible for drafting the reports and the renewals on those grants in YR-4 and YR-3, and I believe the report in YR-2. David's comments regarding Professor Williams's work on the DOE grants are mentioned in her Tenure Review Panel Report of May YR-2. (See Exhibit 10) In May of YR-3 Professor Williams was promoted to the rank of Associate Professor and according to the promotion letter which was copied to me as the Chair of the Tenurial Faculty (See Exhibit 6), she was on track for tenure the next year. Professor Williams was a fine teacher and her scholarship was well regarded. In particular, her *Conwell University Journal of Contemporary Public Problems* is considered the seminal piece in that area of scholarship and frequently cited throughout our academy of public policy professionals.

It was also in the spring of YR-3 that I heard that Professor Williams had become personally involved with David. When I learned this I did warn her to take care in light of David's apparent vindictiveness towards women with whom he had or attempted to have sexual relationships. Professor Williams assured me the relationship with David was a genuine and serious one and that I shouldn't worry. I worried nonetheless.

In the fall of YR-3 I learned that Mary Anne had been offered the Associate Director's position at the Patterson Institute that was coming open in the Spring YR-2. The then-Associate Director Judith Harriman had accepted a position at the Director of the Wiseman Public Policy Institute at Conwell University where she would also assume the Wiseman Chair. It was a great move for Judith and opened a terrific opportunity for Mary Anne. Yes, I'm aware of Judith's untimely death; it was a shock and a tragedy; so young and so talented. The only condition of the associate directorship offer was that Mary Anne receive tenure in YR-2, which seemed, at that point to be a foregone conclusion. I know that Mary Anne was ecstatic about the offer and that she purchased a new condominium in Nita City in anticipation of the added income of the associate director's position and the security of tenure. Howard and I attended her house-warming party.

As I feared the relationship between Professor Williams and David ended. I believe it was in January of YR-2. As I understand it from conversations with Professor Williams, Mary Anne ended the relationship when David failed to fulfill his promise of leaving his wife. I can't say I was surprised at either occurrence. I don't believe that David will ever leave Kathryn. He loves the prestige of the relationship; Kathryn's family has been in Nita City for many generations and is very well regarded. In fact, David and Kathryn live in her family home on University Drive, just down the block from Howard and me. I also know that once David's intentions became clear that Mary Anne would not be involved with a married man. No, I am unaware of any other relationships she might have had with a married man or otherwise. We really didn't talk of such things.

I am aware that Mary Anne took the break up very hard. She was hurt and angry. And in that hurt and anger she said some things that she probably shouldn't have about David's academic honesty. Granted, nothing she said about doing a lot of work that came out under David's name was untrue, but that, unfortunately is the way in the world of grants, even in an academic institution. It is understood that the nominal "primary investigator" will often farm out the work to others who are paid under the grant, whose work will not be acknowledged specifically, and certainly not as an author, even if the writing is theirs. I have never been fond of the practice, it smacks of plagiarism, but it is a reality. Mary Anne's comments about David personally were, in fact, more than warranted, but as it turned out equally damaging to her career. Mary Anne's statements about David's personal and professional integrity, made to numbers of faculty members, particularly upset David, and he said so to me in an attempt to quiet Mary Anne down. In the end, Mary Anne's speaking her mind gave Dean Jefferson the excuse she needed to attempt to legitimize her illegitimate decision to thwart the faculty vote and essentially veto Professor Williams's tenure. Yes, I've seen Jefferson's letter to Professor Williams. It accurately reflects that Professor Williams did not publish an article she expected to be in print by the time of the vote and that her teaching evaluations were lower than her norm. (See Exhibit 15) But Professor Williams was, on balance, equally qualified as Professor Vasquez as reflected in his Tenure Report (Exhibit 13), who deservedly received a favorable tenure vote and was recommended by Jefferson and approved by the University for tenure.

As to the failure to produce new grant money, renewal money which Professor Williams was responsible for in every meaningful way as the author of the DOE grant on privatization of public schools report and renewal application, spends as well as new money. If the renewal is not granted the University gets no new funding and Professor Williams was responsible for that funding. She has brought significantly more dollars to the University than Professor Vasquez who is considered an excellent grantsman.

The collegiality point is, of course, given David's actions and Mary Anne's unfortunate but understandable reaction, unfair and in my mind a subterfuge for Jefferson doing David's bidding, which, I am sure also feeds the University's interest for receiving further money from David's crony, Gregory Patterson and his family's foundation that he controls. Yes, as I said, Exhibit 1 is the official statement of the University standards for tenure, and yes, collegiality is part of being a productive member of the University community and the long term interests of the University. Yet, with the exception of Professor Williams's understandable upset with Simonson, she was an excellent colleague and supportive of the school and the University. It is also true that pursuant to the University policy (See Exhibit 1), the dean of the school involved has an independent responsibility on tenure decisions. I just don't believe this is a situation where Dean Jefferson should have exercised her authority to overturn the will of the faculty; especially given the thinly veiled influence of Simonson in all of this.

In Spring YR-2, after receiving Professor Williams's Tenure Report (Exhibit 10) I was approached by Professor Judith Harriman who wanted to talk to me about Professor Williams's candidacy for tenure. She spoke about the turmoil that Professor Williams's statements about Simonson after their break up was causing. She also pointed out that Professor Williams's class evaluations were lower than usual (in the mid-7s as opposed to her usual mid-8s or better) and that she had missed a publication deadline on a significant article for the *American Public Policy Review*. She suggested to me that perhaps it would be wise for Mary Anne to put her tenure vote off for a year which was her right. She did say that as a result that Mary Anne would not be eligible for the Associate Director's position at the Patterson Institute, but that she thought it was in Mary Anne's interest to put the tenure decision over, repair her reputation as a teacher, scholar and colleague and come up the next year. Yes, I am aware that Professor Binder, who was the dissenter on the

Williams Tenure Report was a candidate for the associate director's job and eventually got it when Mary Anne did not get tenure but I can't say one thing had to do with the other.

I admit that Professor Harriman's analysis of the situation was cogent and that the advice she proposed wise, but I was fairly certain that Mary Anne wouldn't go for it. Nonetheless we had a meeting with Professor Williams and made the suggestion. I also put the offer to put her tenure vote off until YR-1 in writing as part of my duties as the Chair of the Tenurial Faculty. (See Exhibit 11.) As predicted, although she didn't reject the idea out of hand, Professor Williams insisted on coming up for tenure in June YR-2 (See Exhibit 12).

The tenurial faculty considered two candidates for tenure. Professor Vasquez was voted tenure by a near-unanimous vote, and deservedly so. His Tenure Review Report is Exhibit 13. Although there was little debate, Professor Williams's supporters noted her history of fine teaching and scholarship and her excellent work at the Patterson Institute in assisting to get grant renewals and her detractors pointed out the lower-than-normal class evaluations, her missing a *American Public Policy Review* deadline, and the failure to attract new money to the department. It was not a heated debate. In the end, the faculty voted in favor of tenure by a vote of 15–12, with Simonson abstaining. In my opinion it was not improper for him to abstain. Although Jefferson and Simonson did not appear happy about the outcome, I assumed that the question was over and that a tenure recommendation would be made and for the reasons I stated earlier I was appalled when Jefferson essentially vetoed Mary Anne's tenure. No, Jefferson did not speak with me before taking her inappropriate stance. As a courtesy, because I am the Chair of the Tenurial Faculty, one would have expected a consult, but it never happened.

Understandably, Mary Anne took the news very hard. She was obviously distraught and emotionally upset by the whole event. Even though she was given the option of staying on through the Fall YR-2 term, she declined. I talked to her several times over the next six months and at first she seemed very depressed. I know that she applied for faculty positions all over the country and I did what I could for her. Exhibit 24 is the letter I wrote for her. Unfortunately she was unsuccessful in finding another faculty position. Yes, she did show me Exhibits 22 and 23, the letters from Simonson and Jefferson that apparently were sent out from the University. I do not agree with them and although they are not negative in a direct way, they essentially damn with faint praise. These letters would be viewed by any academic committee as unfavorable and I'm sure they were intended as such by Jefferson and Simonson. Their meaning is quite clear.

By Spring YR-1 it became clear that Mary Anne would need to look outside academe for employment. I know she applied to several think tanks and eventually caught on with the Beecher Institute in Nita City. I was able to help her in getting that position. Exhibit 25 is my recommendation letter. Rose Clemmons, Director of the Beecher Institute, is an old and dear friend and colleague. The Beecher Institute received its initial funding from the same foundation that provided the funds for the chair that I hold and the University and the Beecher Institute have a long and cordial relationship with many of our professors, including myself, having acted as consultants to the Beecher Institute over the years.

Mary Anne has been doing a great job in her new position as a senior researcher and I'm sure she will thrive intellectually. I know she is also teaching at Nita Community College. The chances of her ever obtaining a full-time tenure line faculty position at the University level are unfortunately very slim. Given her denial of tenure, the paper trail created by the Simonson and Jefferson letters and the availability of talented young Ph.Ds every year, I think her career will remain in a think-tank atmosphere and perhaps in government.

Mary Anne continues to be a friend and we have agreed to work on a paper together in the future. She was extremely depressed over this whole incident for more than a year and it wasn't until fall YR-1 that she started to seem like herself again. I know she misses her teaching, her students, her colleagues, and her University career terribly. But recently she became engaged to marry a young man named Tom Fisher and I am very happy for her in that regard. I am very sorry this has all occurred. I am embarrassed for the University and the Public Policy School. My relationship with David Simonson will never be a good one again. If I were a younger man I would consider leaving the University for another position. It will take years for us to get over the bad feelings that Jefferson and Simonson have generated. I am also afraid that this incident will have a bad effect on our recruiting bright young women to this faculty. The world of academics is a small one and bad reputations can easily arise from situations like this, and once an institution obtains such a reputation it is hard to overcome.

I have read this deposition and it is complete and accurate.

Marvin Taylor

Subscribed and sworn before me this 18th day of March, YR-0

Harold Potts

Certified Shorthand Reporter

This deposition was given under oath at the offices of the plaintiff's counsel on March 18, YR-0.

Exhibit 1

NITA UNIVERSITY TENURE STANDARDS AND PROCEDURES

A. PREAMBLE

TENURE SHALL BE BASED ON A DETERMINATION THAT A FACULTY MEMBER WILL CONTRIBUTE SUBSTANTIALLY TO THE UNIVERSITY, HAS MET THE ACCEPTED STANDARDS FOR SCHOLARSHIP, TEACHING, AND SERVICE AND HAS SHOWN EVIDENCE OF OUTSTANDING PERFORMANCE WITH RESPECT TO TWO OF THESE THREE CATEGORIES, AND EVIDENCE OF EXCELLENT PERFORMANCE WITH RESPECT TO ANY CATEGORY IN WHICH THERE IS NOT EVIDENCE OF OUTSTANDING PERFORMANCE.

B. STANDARDS

1. **SCHOLARSHIP.** The faculty member must have demonstrated a clear commitment to continuing scholarly achievement by the authorship and publication of at least two professional pieces. A piece which has not yet been published may only be considered if it is completed and accepted for publication. At least one of the pieces of professional scholarship must demonstrate analytical, independent and original thought and must contribute to the faculty member's field by developing the faculty member's unique ideas and insights.

2. **TEACHING.** The faculty member must be an effective teacher. Effective teaching involves mastery of the subject area, familiarity with current developments, the ability to organize material, the ability to convey material, and the capacity to inspire the intellect of the faculty member's students. Teaching shall be evaluated on the basis of classroom performance as evidenced by student and peer evaluations.

3. **SERVICE.** The faculty member must demonstrate the ability and willingness to perform appropriate service to the faculty member's school and to the University at large. In appropriate disciplines, service includes the demonstrated independent ability to attract and secure funding for the University from outside sources to assist in supporting the mission of the University.

C. PROCEDURES

1. In order to be eligible for tenure the faculty member must be in the sixth or seventh year of service as a full-time Presidential faculty member. The faculty member may then request consideration for tenure.

2. In order to be eligible for tenure the faculty member must receive a positive majority vote of the tenurial faculty in the faculty member's School certifying that the above stated standards

have been met. The failure of the tenurial faculty of the faculty member's School to make the required certification for tenure by a majority vote is not reviewable, nor is reconsideration available.

3. In order to be eligible for tenure the faculty member must receive the positive recommendation of the Dean of the faculty member's School certifying that the above stated standards have been met. In addition, the Dean of the faculty member's School must make an affirmative finding that the tenure of the faculty member is in the long term best interests of the University. The failure of the Dean of the faculty member's School to make a positive recommendation on tenure is not reviewable nor is reconsideration available

4. If the faculty member receives the required certification for tenure from the tenurial faculty of the faculty member's School <u>and</u> the required recommendation for tenure from the Dean of the faculty member's School, the certification and recommendation shall be submitted to the University Board of Trustees for its independent approval. Approval of tenure for a faculty member shall be based on an affirmative finding of the University Board of Trustees that the tenure of the faculty member is in the long term interests of the University. The failure of the University Board of Trustees to approve the tenure of the faculty member is not reviewable nor is reconsideration available.

5. If the faculty member fails to achieve the positive certification of the tenurial faculty of the faculty member's School, the recommendation of the Dean of the faculty member's School or the approval of tenure by the University Board of Trustees as set out above, the faculty member's service with the University shall be terminated at the end of the semester in which such a failure occurs. At the discretion of the Dean of the faculty member's School, the faculty member may remain in the employ of the University for one semester following a negative determination on tenure.

ADOPTED
Nita University Board of Trustees
January 15, YR-10

Exhibit 2

Mary Anne Williams, Ph.D.
RESUME

EDUCATION:

B.A. Public Policy, Northwestern University, Evanston, Illinois
Magna Cum Laude, June YR-11

Ph.D. Public Policy, Duke University Sanford School of Public Policy
Durham, North Carolina Magna Cum Laude, June YR-8

EMPLOYMENT:

Senior Researcher, Beecher Institute, Nita City, Nita, YR-1 to present
Associate Professor, Nita University School of Public Policy
Nita City, Nita, YR-3–YR-2

Assistant Professor, Nita University School of Public Policy
Nita City, Nita, YR-8–YR-3

Researcher, Patterson Institute for Public Policy, Nita University,
Nita City, Nita YR-6–YR-3

PUBLICATIONS:

"Public School Privatization: Not Now, Not Ever"
American Public Policy Review, October YR-2

Report and Renewal Application on Department of Education Project on Public School Privatization, (Draft prepared for and adopted in whole by David Simonson) July YR-4 and July YR-3, July YR-2 (Report Only) resulting in annual funding of $450,000

"Unequal Funding for Inner City Schools: Is Privatization am Answer?"
Conwell University Journal of Contemporary Public Problems,
November YR-4

"The Public School Mess: Unequal Funding for the Inner City,"
Nita State University Journal of Public Policy, April YR-6

PERSONAL:

Address:	115 Winding Way, Nita City, Nita
Phone:	(989) 225-8482
E-mail:	MAW@aom.com
References:	On request

Exhibit 3

NITA UNIVERSITY

356 University Drive Nita City, Nita 69999

School of Public Policy Office of the Dean

David A. Simonson, Dean

February 10, YR-8
Dr. Mary Anne Williams
1400 Hillgrand Avenue
Durham, North Carolina 27705

Dear Dr. Williams:

I am delighted on behalf of Nita University to offer you a position as Assistant Professor in the School of Public Policy commencing in the Fall Semester YR-8. The offer is made without tenure and will be based on a twelve-month contract renewable on agreement of you and the University each year.

The beginning salary with be $50,000 for the YR-8–YR-7 academic year. Salary will be renegotiated with each succeeding contract. In addition you will receive the full range of University benefits with a value calculated at 27 percent of base salary as described in the University benefits brochure that has been previously supplied to you.

You will be assigned courses to teach at the discretion of the Dean, but in no event will you be required to teach more than fifteen credits in any academic year. In addition you will be expected to produce acceptable scholarship on a continuing basis and perform appropriate University service.

You will be eligible for promotion to the rank of Associate Professor in YR-3 and eligible for tenure in YR-2. The standards for tenure are set out in the attachment to this letter.

MAW

Initials

2/14/YR-8

Date

If all of the above is acceptable to you, please indicate the same by signing, initialing, and returning one copy of this letter to me no later than March 15, YR-8.

Congratulations and welcome.

Sincerely:

David A. Simonson
Dean

Enclosure:

Accepted:

Mary Anne Williams, Ph.D.

2/14/YR-8

Date

Exhibit 4A

NITA UNIVERSITY

School of Public Policy Office of the Dean
356 University Drive   Nita City, Nita 69999

Christine Jefferson, Dean

DATE: May 15, YR-7
TO: Professor Mary Anne Williams
FROM: Dean Christine Jefferson
RE: Yearly Review

I am pleased to provide you with the following review of your performance as an Assistant Professor in the School of Public Policy for Academic Year YR-8–YR-7.

I. Teaching—

A. **Course Load—**You have been assigned to teach fourteen credits for the past academic year.

B. **Teaching Evaluations—**you have been evaluated by your students and faculty colleagues as shown below. All numerical rankings are on a ten-point scale and have been averaged for all of your courses unless there is cause for concern in a particular course in which event the ratings for that course are listed separately.

1. Student Evaluations—

a.	Mastery of Subject	6.4
b.	Current Developments	6.8
c.	Organization	6.9
d.	Conveying Material	6.2
e.	Intellectual Inspiration	6.0
f.	Overall Effectiveness	6.1

2. Faculty Evaluations—No formal evaluations

II. Scholarship—No publications. Work progressing on first article regarding funding of public education for inner city schools. Publication expected Spring YR-6.

III. Service—Assigned to Curriculum Committee for P.P.S. Advisor to Debate Society.

IV. Dean's Comment—Acceptable first year. Meets all expectations. Class evaluations well within acceptable range. Need to focus on scholarship for YR-7–YR-6 academic year.

V. Salary for YR-8–YR-6—$51,500 which represents average raise for School of 3 percent.

Exhibit 4B

NITA UNIVERSITY

School of Public Policy Office of the Dean
356 University Drive Nita City, Nita 69999

Christine Jefferson, Dean

DATE: May 16, YR-6
TO: Professor Mary Anne Williams
FROM: Dean Christine Jefferson
RE: Yearly Review

I am pleased to provide you with the following review of your performance as an Assistant Professor in the School of Public Policy for Academic Year YR-7–YR-6.

I. Teaching—

A. Course Load—You have been assigned to teach fourteen credits for the past academic year.

B. Teaching Evaluations—You have been evaluated by your students and faculty colleagues as shown below. All numerical rankings are on a ten-point scale and have been averaged for all your courses.

1. Student Evaluations—

a.	Mastery of Subject	6.4
b.	Current Developments	6.9
c.	Organization	6.3
d.	Conveying Material	6.3
e.	Intellectual Inspiration	6.0
f.	Overall Effectiveness	6.3

2. Faculty Evaluations—No formal evaluations

II. Scholarship—Published article entitled "The Public School Mess: Unequal Funding for the Inner City" in the *Nita State University Journal of Public Policy* Spring YR-6 issue. Will begin work this summer on more expansive article in the same area.

III. Service—Curriculum Committee, Graduate Placement Committee (P.P.S.) Alumni Fund Raising Committee (University). Advisor to Debate Society.

IV. Dean's Comment—Excellent first publication; mainly descriptive. Next article needs more analysis and original thought. Teaching evaluations acceptable. A little flat when compared to previous year. Expect improvement in teaching evaluations next year. Faculty visits scheduled for Academic Year YR-6–YR-5.

V. Salary for YR-6–YR-5—$54,075 which represents school high percentage raise of 5 percent.

Exhibit 4C

NITA UNIVERSITY

School of Public Policy Office of the Dean

356 University Drive Nita City, Nita 69999

Christine Jefferson, Dean

DATE: May 17, YR-5
TO: Professor Mary Anne Williams
FROM: Dean Christine Jefferson
RE: Yearly Review

The following is a review of your academic performance as an Assistant Professor in the School of Public Policy for Academic Year YR-6–YR-5.

I. **Teaching—**

A. **Course Load—**You have been assigned to teach sixteen credits for the past academic year which represents a one-credit overload for which you have been compensated.

B. **Teaching Evaluations—**You have been evaluated by your students and faculty colleagues as shown below. All numerical rankings are on a ten-point scale and have been averaged for all of your courses.

1. Student Evaluations and Faculty Evaluations—

		Students	*Faculty*
a.	Mastery of Subject	7.0	7.0
b.	Current Developments	7.0	7.2
c.	Organization	7.1	7.3
d.	Conveying Material	7.1	7.0
e.	Intellectual Inspiration	7.2	6.8
f.	Overall Effectiveness	7.1	6.9

II. **Scholarship—**Work progressing on article on public school financing with suggestions on how to address the apparent disparity between inner city and suburban schools within the same governmental unit. Article should be enhanced by work as researcher at Patterson Institute for Public Policy. Needs to show more analysis and original thought than first article.

III. **Service—**Curriculum, Graduate Placement Committees (P.P.S.); Alumni Fund Raising Committee (University); Advisor to Debate Society; Advisor to William Royerson, graduate student, on Masters Thesis; working on DOE grant renewal on Privatization of Public Schools under supervision of Professor Simonson.

IV. **Deans Comment—**Improvement in teaching. One faculty member of three person visiting group believes too much spoon feeding in courses. Suggests challenging students intellectually in a more aggressive way. Some serious questions raised regarding collegiality from other members of University Alumni Fund Raising Committee.

V. **Salary for YR-5–YR-4—**$56,238 which represents high/average raise for School of 4 percent.

Exhibit 4D

NITA UNIVERSITY
School of Public Policy Office of the Dean
356 University Drive Nita City, Nita 69999

Christine Jefferson, Dean

DATE: May 14, YR-4
TO: Professor Mary Anne Williams
FROM: Dean Christine Jefferson
RE: Yearly Review

The following is a review of your academic performance as an Assistant Professor in the School of Public Policy for Academic Year YR-5–YR-4.

I. **Teaching—**

A. **Course Load—**You have been assigned to teach sixteen credits for the past academic year which represents a one-credit overload for which you have been compensated.

B. **Teaching Evaluations—**You have been evaluated by your students and faculty colleagues as shown below. All numerical rankings are on a ten-point scale and have been averaged for all of your courses.

1. Student Evaluations and Faculty Evaluations

		Students	*Faculty*
a.	Mastery of Subject	7.5	7.8
b.	Current Developments	8.2	8.4
c.	Organization	7.9	8.0
d.	Conveying Material	8.1	8.1
e.	Intellectual Inspiration	8.3	7.7
f.	Overall Effectiveness	8.2	8.1

II. **Scholarship—**Article entitled "Unequal Funding for Inner City Schools: Is Privatization an Answer?" has been accepted for publication in the *Conwell University Journal of Contemporary Public Problems*, Fall YR-4 Issue which is a faculty edited journal.

III. **Service—**Curriculum, Graduate Student Placement, Alumni Fund Raising Committees (P.P.S.), Faculty Senate Representative (University), successful renewal application for DOE grant to Patterson Institute in Summer YR-5, preparing renewal for YR-4.

IV. **Dean's Comment—**Teaching evaluations up nicely. One faculty reviewer believes still some spoon feeding. Accepted publication is in excellent peer reviewed journal. Reviewed by Professor Taylor who comments favorably. On track for promotion to Associate Professor in spring of YR-3.

V. **Salary for YR-4–YR-3—**$58,487 which represents high/average raise for School of 4 percent.

Exhibit 4E

NITA UNIVERSITY

School of Public Policy Office of the Dean
356 University Drive Nita City, Nita 69999

Christine Jefferson, Dean

DATE: May 16, YR-3
TO: Professor Mary Anne Williams
FROM: Dean Christine Jefferson
RE: Yearly Review

The following is a review of your academic performance as an Assistant Professor in the School of Public Policy for Academic Year YR-4–YR-3.

I. **Teaching—**

A. **Course Load—**You have been assigned to teach sixteen credits for the past academic year which represents a one-credit overload for which you have been compensated.

B. **Teaching Evaluations—**You have been evaluated by your students and faculty colleagues as shown below. All numerical rankings are on a ten-point scale and have been averaged for all of your courses.

1. Student Evaluations and Faculty Evaluations—

		Students	*Faculty*
a.	Mastery of Subject	8.5	8.5
b.	Current Developments	8.3	8.4
c.	Organization	8.0	8.3
d.	Conveying Material	8.5	8.4
e.	Intellectual Inspiration	8.5	8.3
f.	Overall Effectiveness	8.4	8.5

II. **Scholarship—**Published article entitled "Unequal Funding for Inner City Schools: Is Privatization an Answer?" in the *Conwell University Journal of Contemporary Public Problems*, Fall YR-4 issue. Article received universal approval from faculty. Professors Simonson and Taylor give article high marks. Solicited by *American Public Policy Review* to participate in issue dedicated to "The Public School Crisis" scheduled for Spring YR-2.

III. **Service—**Curriculum, Graduate Student Scholarship, Alumni Fund Raising Committees (P.P.S.) Faculty Senate Representative (University) Professor Simonson reports Professor Williams major contributor on DOE grant which has generated $450,000 annually for University through Patterson Institute beginning in YR-6.

IV. **Dean's Comment—**On track for tenure. Scholarship excellent. *APPR* article for Spring YR-3 a real plus. Teaching excellent. Promoted to Associate Professor by a unanimous faculty vote and recommendation of Dean.

V. **Salary for YR-3–YR-2—**$70,000 which represents high raise for School of 5 percent plus increment for promotion.

Exhibit 5A

PIPP

The Patterson Institute for Public Policy

Nita University
Nita City, Nita

July 1, YR-6

Mary Anne Williams
Assistant Professor
Nita University School of Public Policy
Nita City, Nita 99999

Dear Professor Williams:

It is with great pleasure that I appoint you as a Researcher at the Patterson Institute for Public Policy for Academic Year YR-6–YR-5. You will be assigned various tasks consistent with the work and mission of the Patterson Institute which will include research, data compilation, drafting of reports on Institute projects, and drafting of grant applications and renewals. It is expected that for the immediate future your primary responsibility will be to work on a U.S. Department of Education Grant on Public School Privatization under my supervision. Your stipend for Academic Year YR-6–YR-5 will be $9,000.

Welcome aboard. I am sure you will find the work of the Patterson Institute challenging and rewarding.

Sincerely,

David A. Simonson, Ph.D.
Director
Patterson Professor of Public Policy
Nita University

Exhibit 5B

PIPP

The Patterson Institute for Public Policy

Nita University
Nita City, Nita

July 1, YR-5

Mary Anne Williams
Assistant Professor
Nita University School of Public Policy
Nita City, Nita 99999

Dear Professor Williams:

It is with great pleasure that I appoint you as a Researcher at the Patterson Institute for Public Policy for Academic Year YR-5–YR-4. You will be assigned various tasks consistent with the work and mission of the Patterson Institute which will include research, data compilation, drafting of reports on Institute projects, and drafting of grant applications and renewals. Your stipend for Academic Year YR-5–YR-4 will be $9,800.

I look forward to another productive year.

Sincerely,

David A. Simonson

David A. Simonson, Ph.D.
Director
Patterson Professor of Public Policy
Nita University

Exhibit 5C

PIPP

The Patterson Institute for Public Policy

Nita University
Nita City, Nita

July 1, YR-4

Mary Anne Williams
Assistant Professor
Nita University School of Public Policy
Nita City, Nita 99999

Dear Professor Williams:

It is with great pleasure that I appoint you as a Researcher at the Patterson Institute for Public Policy for Academic Year YR-4–YR-3. You will be assigned various tasks consistent with the work and mission of the Patterson Institute which will include research, data compilation, drafting of reports on Institute projects, and drafting of grant applications and renewals. Your stipend for Academic Year YR-4–YR-3 will be $10,500.

I look forward to another productive year.

Sincerely,

David A. Simonson, Ph.D.
Director
Patterson Professor of Public Policy
Nita University

Exhibit 5D

PIPP

The Patterson Institute for Public Policy

Nita University
Nita City, Nita

July 1, YR-3

Mary Anne Williams
Assistant Professor
Nita University School of Public Policy
Nita City, Nita 99999

Dear Professor Williams:

Congratulations on your promotion to Associate Professor. It is well deserved, especially in light of your excellent work at the Patterson Institute on our Department of Education grant on public school privatization on which you have been instrumental in obtaining our past two renewals. As you know, that grant has generated $450,000 annually for the past several years in support of the Institute and the University.

It is my pleasure to once again appoint you as a Researcher at the Patterson Institute for Public Policy for Academic Year YR-3–YR-2. Your duties will be the same as in the past, although I will be relying on you to take on some increased administrative responsibilities consistent with your tenure at the Institute.

Your stipend for Academic Year YR-3–YR-2 will be $11,500.

Sincerely,

David A. Simonson

David A. Simonson, Ph.D.
Director
Patterson Professor of Public Policy
Nita University

cc: Dean Christine Jefferson
Nita University
School of Public Policy

Exhibit 6

NITA UNIVERSITY
356 University Drive Nita City, Nita 69999

School of Public Policy Office of the Dean
Christine Jefferson, Dean

June 1, YR-3

Professor Mary Anne Williams
Nita University
School of Public Policy
Nita City, Nita 99999

Dear Professor Williams:

It is with a great deal of pride and pleasure that I write to inform you, that by a unanimous vote of the tenurial faculty, my certification, and approval by the President of the University that you have been promoted to the rank of Associate Professor, without tenure, in the School of Public Policy. This promotion is effective for Academic Year YR-3–YR-2 beginning July 1, YR-3.

A you know from receipt of your written Yearly Review, we are very pleased with your development as one of our finest young teachers and scholars. Your most recent article in the *Conwell University Journal of Contemporary Public Problems* shows the kind of analytical, independent and original work offering unique ideas and insights that are the hallmark of scholarly production at the University level. We look forward to your upcoming article in the Symposium Issue on "The Public School Crisis" of the *APPR* scheduled for next spring. Last, but certainly not the least, we are most pleased with your contributions to the Patterson Institute in terms of work product and attracting much needed and appreciated grant renewal funds to the University.

Although obviously no commitments can be made, you know of my opinion that you are on track for tenure in the spring of YR-2 and I see no reason, at the present time, why the process should be anything but favorable for you, the School, and the University.

Congratulations on your many professional achievements and your promotion. We expect great things from you in the future.

Sincerely,

Christine Jefferson

Christine Jefferson, Dean
School of Public Policy
cc: Marvin Taylor
Beecher Professor of Public Policy

Exhibit 7

PIPP

The Patterson Institute for Public Policy

Nita University
Nita City, Nita

October 12, YR-3

Mary Anne Williams, Ph.D.
Associate Professor, Nita University
School of Public Policy
Nita City, Nita 99999

Dear Professor Williams:

It is with great pleasure that I write to offer you the position of Associate Director of the Patterson Institute for Public Policy commencing on July 1, YR-2. Congratulations. You have been selected from a distinguished list of applicants in recognition of your outstanding record in the Nita University School of Public Policy as a teacher and a scholar and your excellent work in the funding and execution of the various projects of the Patterson Institute.

Your contract for this position will be on a year-to-year basis and will be renegotiated each year between you and the Institute. It is anticipated that as you gain experience as the Associate Director that your compensation will be increased accordingly consistent with available funding. Your stipend as Associate Director for Academic Year YR-2–YR-1 will be $24,000.

The only condition of this offer is that you receive tenure in the School of Public Policy on or before July 1, YR-2, the commencement date of this appointment. In light of your record at the University I do not anticipate that this condition will present any impediment to your assuming the Associate Director's position.

If this offer is acceptable to you please indicate the same by signing and initialing one copy of this letter and returning it to me no later than November 15, YR-3.

MAW

Initials

10/15/YR-3

Date

Welcome to your new and exciting position.

Warm regards,

David A. Simonson, Ph.D.
Director
Patterson Professor of Public Policy
Nita University

Mary Anne Williams, Ph.D

10/15/YR-3
Date

cc: Dean Christine Jefferson
Nita University
School of Public Policy

Exhibit 8

PIPP

The Patterson Institute for Public Policy

Nita University
Nita City, Nita

From the desk of
Judith Harriman

CONFIDENTIAL

Date: March 3, YR-2

To: Mary Anne Williams

From: Judith Harriman

Re: Your Current Workload

Mary Anne, I am writing to encourage you to bring more attention and energy to your work at the Institute. In reviewing the projects on which you are assigned, it appears that you are falling behind on some of your work.

I know that you have been going through what I assume will be a short-term rough period, but it's now time to get yourself together and once again return to the high level of production that we have come to expect from you.

This a personal concern on my part. I know that David is still behind your appointment to the Associate Director's position, as am I, but you need to get back on track so as to avoid any long-term potential problems.

On a personal note, if I can be of any assistance to you please let me know. I know that you have been upset recently and I have a long-term relationship with a professional counselor who may be of assistance to you in getting over this bump in the road. Let me know.

Exhibit 9

THE AMERICAN PUBLIC POLICY REVIEW

12 PARK COURT NEW • YORK, NEW YORK

April 10, YR-2

Professor Mary Anne Williams
Nita University
School of Public Policy
Nita City, Nita 99997

Dear Professor Williams:

We are most disappointed that you will be unable to complete your article on public school privatization in time for our symposium issue on "The Public School Crisis" scheduled for Spring YR-2. It will be missed.

As you know, we needed to receive the article by April 1, YR-2 in order to meet our publication deadline and are unable to grant any extensions, for any reason. I understand from our conversation that you have been experiencing some scheduling problems on your many commitments, but unfortunately we just have no leeway.

We are still interested in your article although it obviously would have been best placed in the Spring Symposium. I believe that I may have an opening in the Fall YR-2 issue if that interests you. I will know within a month whether there is room in that issue depending on your article's length.

Thank you for your interest in our publication. I look forward to further communication with you.

Sincerely:

David R. Wellman

David R. Wellman
Editor in Chief

Exhibit 10

NITA UNIVERSITY

356 University Drive Nita City, Nita 69999

School of Public Policy

DATE: May 5, YR-2

TO: Tenurial Faculty
Professor Marvin Taylor, Chair

FROM: Professors Binder, Epstein, and Cooley (Chair)
Tenurial Panel for Professor Mary Anne Williams

RE: Tenure Report for Professor Mary Anne Williams

The Tenurial Panel for Associate Professor Mary Anne Williams, consisting of Professors James Binder, Roger Epstein, and John Cooley submits this report for consideration by the Tenurial Faculty. The Panel, by a vote of 2–1 (Professor Binder dissenting in part) recommends that Professor Mary Anne Williams be granted tenure at the rank of Associate Professor.

I. MAJORITY REPORT

Professor Williams came to the Nita University School of Public Policy faculty after receiving her B.A. in Public Policy from Northwestern University and her Ph.D. in Public Policy from the Sanford School of Public Policy of Duke University.

As her attached Yearly Reports show she has made steady and consistent progress in her career as an academic. As a result of a careful examination of her teaching evaluations, her scholarship, and her service record the majority of this Panel concludes that Professor Williams will contribute substantially to the University and has met the accepted standards for scholarship, teaching and service by showing evidence of outstanding performance with respect to teaching and scholarship and evidence of excellent performance with respect to service. As such, Professor Williams meets out standards for tenure as an Associate Professor.

A. Teaching

Professor Williams has made sustained and consistent progress as an instructor and deserves her reputation as a first rate teacher. By her fourth year of teaching in Academic Year YR-5–YR-4 she was rated by both students and faculty in terms of overall effectiveness at the level of 8.2 and 8.1 respectively on the University's ten-point scale, which easily exceeds our traditional 7.5 benchmark for teaching effectiveness. The majority of the panel notes that Professor Williams's overall teaching effectiveness ratings rose to 8.4 (students) and 8.5 (faculty) in Academic Year YR-4–YR-3. Her performance continued at an extremely high level in the Fall Semester YR-3 where her overall effectiveness ratings were

8.7 (students) and 8.7 (faculty). In Spring Semester YR-2 there was a decline to overall effectiveness ratings of 7.8 (students), 7.5 (faculty). The Panel majority views those ratings as aberrational, but still for the academic year, average overall effectiveness ratings are well above what would be considered outstanding performance as a teacher.

The Panel Majority specifically finds Professor Williams has demonstrated evidence of outstanding mastery of her course material, familiarity with current developments in her field, ability to organize material, ability to convey material and the capacity to inspire the intellect of her students. As such, Professor Williams's teaching meets the University's standards for tenure.

B. Scholarship

Professor Williams has published two articles and has completed substantial work on a third. The first article, "The Public School Mess: Unequal funding for the Inner City," was published in the Spring YR-6 issue of the *Nita State University Journal of Public Policy*. This article gathers voluminous amounts of information about funding and funding patterns for public schools in ten city school systems across the country. The article describes the apparent problem of unequal funding in inner city versus suburban public schools in the same school system and relates the differences to differences in standardized test scores. The article is mainly descriptive but makes substantial contributions to the literature in Professor Williams's (then emerging) area of expertise. The Panel majority notes that this article has been cited by virtually every piece of scholarship on this issue since its publication and uses Professor Williams's work as the jumping off point for further in-depth analysis.

Professor Williams's second article, "Unequal Funding For Inner City Schools: Is Privatization an Answer?" was published in the Fall YR-4 issue of the prestigious *Conwell University Journal of Contemporary Public Problems (CJCPP). CJCPP* is a faculty-edited journal and with the exception of the *American Public Policy Review*, it is considered perhaps the top journal in the country for public policy issues. This article proceeds from where Professor Williams's first article leaves off and analyzes the problem, and its causes and inquires as to whether privatization is a potential answer to improving inner city public education in a time of limited resources. Professor ultimately concludes that privatization is not a solution to the problem she originally identified, but suggests a scheme of experimentation so that the possible solution of privatization can be fully explored and its effects studied. This article demonstrates a mature intellect bringing wisdom and insight to a thorny problem. It clearly shows the kind of independent analytical thinking that is the mark of an excellent scholar.

The Panel majority concludes that Professor Williams has demonstrated evidence of outstanding performance with respect to scholarship. Her two articles, taken together, and the fact that she has neared completion on a third article, shows clear continuing scholarly achievement. Her *CJCPP* article demonstrates analytical, independent, and original thought, and demonstrates Professor Williams's unique insights and ideas. Both of her articles contribute significantly to her field of expertise. The Panel majority concludes that Professor Williams's scholarship meets the University's standards for tenure.

C. Service

Professor Williams has served with distinction on a full range of School of Public Policy and University Committees. (See attached Yearly Reports) In addition she has worked as the Advisor to the School's Debate Society and as one of our Representatives on the Faculty Senate. In the ever increasing important role of attracting outside resources to the University, she has done excellent work at the Patterson

Institute, where as reported by Professor Simonson (Director of the Institute), to us on numerous occasions, her work has contributed significantly to obtaining renewals of a Department of Education grant on Public School Privatization that has brought an average of $450,000 per year to the University in the past several years.

In addition, Professor Williams has received an offer to serve as the Associate Director of the Patterson Institute for Public Policy commencing in Academic Year YR-2–YR-1. In that position, and with her growing reputation as an expert in public school resource allocation, the Panel majority is confident that in future years that Professor Williams will be able to independently attract and secure outside funding for University projects.

The Panel majority concludes that Professor Williams has demonstrated evidence of excellent performance in the area of service.

D. Conclusion

Having demonstrated evidence of outstanding performance with regard to teaching and scholarship and evidence of excellent performance with regard to service, the Panel majority concludes that Professor Williams has met the University's standards for tenure at the rank of Associate Professor and therefore recommends that the Tenurial Faculty vote to adopt this conclusion.

RESPECTFULLY SUBMITTED,

Roger Epstein, Ph.D.
Professor of Public Policy

John Cooley, Ph.D.
Professor of Public Policy
Chair

II. DISSENTING REPORT

My dissent is one based on caution, not disagreement. I agree that Professor Williams has been an outstanding teacher and that the scholarship she has completed is of high quality. I am disturbed by the fact that her teaching evaluations took a precipitous dip in the eyes of both students and faculty in the Spring YR-2 semester. I am also disturbed by her failure to meet a publication deadline for an article in the *American Public Policy Review* that would have, assuming the continued high quality she demonstrated in her second article, brought great honor to her and to this School. I agree with the Panel majority that her service on School and University Committees and her work at the Patterson Institute to date has been very well received, but I note—again with caution—that she has been unable to attract funding on her own, having merely worked on renewal applications on one grant that was solicited and obtained by Professor Simonson.

As a result of all of the above, and out of caution, I respectfully suggest that Professor Williams's tenure decision be put over until the spring of YR-1, when, in normal course, she can be considered for tenure. Assuming that her teaching this past semester was, as the majority states, aberrational, that she completes and publishes another article of high quality, and that she can perhaps attract some independent funding for the Patterson Institute, the school or the University, she should be voted tenure with the same ease with which she was promoted. I urge, therefore, that the Chair of the Tenurial Faculty communicate my concern through this report or otherwise to Professor Williams, and hope that she accepts my well-meaning and respectful recommendation to reserve her consideration for tenure until Spring YR-1.

RESPECTFULLY SUBMITTED,

James Binder, Ph.D.
Associate Professor of Public Policy

cc: Professor Mary Anne Williams
Dean Christine Jefferson

Exhibit 11

NITA UNIVERSITY

356 University Drive Nita City, Nita 69999

Nita University School of Public Policy
Marvin Taylor, Ph.D., Beecher Professor of Public Policy

May 20, YR-2

Professor Mary Anne Williams
Nita University
School of Public Policy
Nita City, Nita 99999

Dear Professor Williams:

I am writing in my capacity as the Chair of the Tenurial Faculty of the Nita University School of Public Policy.

As you know, your tenure review resulted in a report recommending tenure with one of the three committee members dissenting. The dissenting committee member, although favorably disposed to your tenure based on your history with the school, expressed concern over your recent performance. Notably, the fact that you missed the publication deadline on your much anticipated article planned for the Spring Issue of the *American Public Policy Review*.

It was his suggestion that you put off your tenure consideration for a year until Spring YR-1, at which time, assuming your return to your norm in teaching performance, and the publication of your soon to be completed article, your tenure, at least in his opinion (an opinion I share) will be virtually assured. As you know, pursuant to University policy, a tenure vote for a faculty member in her sixth year as a Presidential appointee is not required.

Please accept this letter as an official offer to put over your tenure consideration until Spring YR-1. This decision is completely yours. We will, of course, abide by whatever decision you reach.

Sincerely:

Marvin Taylor, Ph.D.
Beecher Professor of Public Policy

cc: Dean Christine Jefferson

Exhibit 12

NITA UNIVERSITY
356 University Drive Nita City, Nita 69999

Nita University School of Public Policy
Mary Anne Williams, Ph.D.
Associate Professor

May 24, YR-2

Marvin Taylor, Ph.D., Chair
Tenurial Faculty
Nita University
School of Public Policy
Nita City, Nita

Sent via—Campus Mail

Dear Professor Taylor:

Thank you for you letter of May 20, YR-2. Although I appreciate your offer, as I told you in person, today, I have decided to go forward on my tenure decision this year.

I believe that the Tenure Panel Majority Report fairly states my history at the University and that my qualifications meet the University standards for tenure. Although the minority report is factually accurate, I believe the conclusions are unwarranted and may be affected by the fact that Professor Binder was a disappointed candidate for the position of Associate Director of the Patterson Institute for Public Policy which was ultimately offered to me and knows, that should I not receive tenure this year, that I would not be eligible for that position.

On a personal note, thank you for all of your support and encouragement.

Warm regards,

Mary Anne Williams

Mary Anne Williams, Ph.D.
Associate Professor

Exhibit 13

NITA UNIVERSITY

356 University Drive Nita City, Nita 69999

School of Public Policy

DATE: May 2, YR-2

TO: Tenurial Faculty
Professor Marvin Taylor, Chair

FROM: Professors Esposito, Graham, and Brownstein (Chair)
Tenurial Panel for Professor Mary Anne Williams

RE: Tenure Report for Professor William Vasquez

The Tenurial Panel for Assistant Professor William Vasquez, consisting of Professors Eleanor Esposito, David Graham, and Howard Brownstein (Chair) submits this report for consideration by the Tenurial Faculty. The Panel unanimously recommends that Professor William Vasquez be granted tenure and promoted to the rank of Associate Professor.

INTRODUCTION

Professor Vasquez is a YR-12 cum laude graduate of Nita State University with a B.A. in Political Science. In YR-9 he received his Ph.D. cum laude, in Public Policy from Conwell University at which point he accepted a position as an Assistant Professor on the faculty of the Nita University School of Public Policy.

As a result of a careful examination of his teaching evaluations and classroom performance, a studied review of his scholarship and an examination of his record of service, the Panel concludes that Professor Vasquez will contribute substantially to the University and has met the accepted standards for teaching, scholarship and service by demonstrating evidence of outstanding performance in scholarship and service and evidence of excellent performance in teaching. As a result, Professor Vasquez meets our standards for tenure as an Associate Professor.

A. Teaching

Professor Vasquez has made consistent progress in his teaching in his time at the University. Although he experienced some difficulty in his early years on faculty, for the past three years he has averaged an overall effectiveness rating of 7.5 from his students and 7.8 from his faculty colleagues. Although these averages are on the low side for acceptable teaching, (7.5 being the benchmark evaluation for acceptable teaching, the panel, after visiting numerous classes, is of the opinion that the ratings are more result of a halting style on the part of Professor Vasquez as opposed to any lack of substance. The Panel further notes that Professor Vasquez has been extremely open to comments and critique from his colleagues and has displayed extraordinary effort in attaining acceptable teaching performances. In his first three years of his time on the faculty, he took advantage of a reduced teaching load of one, two, and three credit underloads so that he could work on his craft. The panel notes that this hard work has paid off in teaching at an acceptable level.

The Panel specifically finds that Professor Vasquez has demonstrated evidence of excellent mastery of his course material, familiarity with current developments in his field, ability to organize material, ability to convey material, and the capacity to inspire the intellect of his students. As such, taken in conjunction with findings contained in the rest of this report, Professor Vasquez's teaching meets the University's standards for tenure at the rank of Associate Professor.

B. **Scholarship**

In his seven years at the University, Professor Vasquez has earned a deserved reputation as a scholar of the first order. He has published four articles and numerous reports on the grants he has garnered for the University (see Service section of this report). In addition, he is nearing completion on a fifth article that will be published in the Fall YR-2 issue of the peer edited and highly regarded *Conwell University Journal of Contemporary Public Problems*.

Professor Vasquez's primary scholarly interest is with regard the issues surrounding the exercise of voting rights by minority populations. His first article, "Where Have All The Voters Gone: A Study of Voting Trends In the United States," was published in the Winter YR-8 issue of the *Columbus University of Nita Journal of Politics*. Typical of early scholarship, it collects a significant amount of data and organizes that data in useful ways. As such, it describes the previous twenty years of voting trends in national elections, concluding, among other things, that there has been a steady decline in the percentage of eligible voters who actually come to the polls for national elections.

Professor Vasquez's second article is a refinement of the first. Entitled "In Search of the Minority Voter," and published in the Spring YR-6 issue of the *Nita State Journal of Public Policy*, this article again collects voluminous information about voting patterns of African American, Asian American, and Hispanic American voters and concludes that the percentage of participation in national elections for these groups is even lower than the population as a whole. This article, like his first, is extremely well researched and written with great precision and clarity in describing the phenomenon born out by the collected statistics, and serves as a jumping off point for two more analytical pieces of writing.

In YR-5 Professor Vasquez published his seminal article on voting patterns and their causes among Hispanic American voters. This article appears in the Spring YR-5 issue of the *Columbia College of Conwell Journal of Civil Liberties*. It takes the information from his earlier work and subjects the data regarding Hispanic American voters to analysis regarding the causes of low voter turnout, tracing its origins to lower socio-economic status for newly naturalized citizens and showing that as populations become more affluent that the likelihood of participating in the electoral process increases. The article concludes that Hispanic American voters who have attained middle class status, economically, are actually more likely to vote than African American, Asian American, or Caucasian voters in the same economic grouping. It was this article, which received national attention that has resulted in Professor Vasquez bringing several grants to the University as described in the section of this report regarding service.

Professor Vasquez's YR-3 article in the Fall YR-3 issue of the *Nita State Journal of Public Policy*, entitled "Dollars and the Voting Booth: Economic Power and the Decision to Vote in Asian American

Populations," updates and refines the data relied upon in his YR-5 article and comes to similar conclusions. This article expands upon the former by performing a similar analysis regarding the Asian American population as he performed earlier with regard to the Hispanic American population. It too, is well researched, well written, and persuasive in the positions taken. This article, too, has received general acceptance for its accuracy and completeness of research and for its analytical precision.

Finally, the Panel comments favorably on the drafts it has reviewed of Professor Vasquez's soon to be published article in the aforementioned CJCPP. Professor Vasquez was solicited to write this article, tentatively entitled, "Enhancing Political Power: A Rush to the Polls," by the editorial board of *CJCPP.* This article discusses the newly emerging phenomenon of Political Action Groups run by Hispanic American interests and funded by businesses owned and operated by Hispanic Americans and their employees. It describes this emerging political power base and examines the issues upon which the Hispanic American population appears to seek to have the greatest influence. Although not yet completed, given the quality of the *Journal* (which answers some earlier faculty criticism that Professor Vasquez had yet to publish in a top-rated journal) and its audience, this article is sure to have significant impact in the academy and otherwise.

Based on all of the above, the Panel specifically finds that the body of Professor Vasquez's work demonstrates analytical, independent and original thought and conveys the author's unique ideas and insights. As such, the Panel concludes that Professor Vasquez has demonstrated evidence of outstanding performance in the area of scholarship and meets the University's standards for tenure at the rank of Associate Professor.

C. **Service**

Professor Vasquez has served with enthusiasm and distinction on a full range of School of Public Policy and University Committees. He has been a long-term member of the Curriculum, Faculty Recruitment, and Admissions Committees at the School. These three Committees, with their enormous required time commitment, are perhaps the most demanding in the school. Professor Vasquez has brought energy, insight, and his unique perspective to the important work of these Committees. In addition, he has served as the faculty advisor to the Hispanic American League of Students for five years in the School, and for the past two years has assumed a similar position with the Hispanic American University Students Organization at the University level. Professor Vazquez has also served as the faculty representative to the University Disciplinary Committee for five years where he was a UDC Judge.

In addition, Professor Vasquez has demonstrated an outstanding ability to attract and secure funding for the University from outside sources. His first grant was obtained from the Bidwell Foundation in 1999 to study voting patterns among Hispanic American voters. This work led to larger grants from the Royalton Foundation and the Hispanic American League in YR-4 and YR-3, with renewals appearing to virtually certain. These grants have brought an average of $150,000 to the University for the past three years, and in the opinion of the Panel, these funding levels are likely to be exceeded in the future from these and other sources.

The Panel concludes that Professor Vasquez has demonstrated evidence of outstanding performance in the area of service and as such has met then University's standards for tenure at the rank of Associate Professor.

D. Conclusion

The Panel concludes unanimously that Professor Vasquez has demonstrated evidence of outstanding performance in the areas of scholarship and service and evidence of excellent performance in the area of teaching, and as such meets the University's standards for tenure at the rank of Associate Professor. The Panel recommends, again unanimously, that the Tenurial Faculty vote to recommend to the University that Professor Vasquez be granted tenure and promoted to the rank of Associate Professor.

Respectfully submitted,

Eleanor Esposito, Ph.D. Associate Professor	David Graham, Ph.D. Professor	Howard Brownstein, Ph.D. Professor (Chair)

cc: Professor William Vasquez
Dean Christine Jefferson
Mary Anne Williams, Ph.D. Associate Professor

Exhibit 14

PIPP

The Patterson Institute for Public Policy

Nita University
Nita City, Nita

Gregory Patterson, Jr.
Chairman

June 8, YR-2

Dean Christine Jefferson
Nita University
School of Public Policy
Nita City, Nita 99999

Dear Christine:

I am writing to report to you some disturbing information that has come to my attention from various sources. I have already spoken to David Simonson about this matter and he has assured me that it is nothing to worry about, but I am not sure that his optimism is well founded.

In the past several months I have been accosted by several well-placed people within the community of charitable foundations who are in a position to be of great assistance to the Patterson Institute, the Public Policy School, and the University as a whole. They have inquired about rumors that have reached them of some, what they termed as "major upheaval" within the Public Policy School. As has been reported to me, a junior member of your faculty, who has gone unnamed (although I suspect you know about whom they are speaking), has made numerous public statements that have been disparaging to David Simonson both personally and professionally, calling into question his personal honesty and his professional integrity.

As I am sure you are aware, David Simonson attracts a great deal of funding to your school and the Patterson Institute, and such rumors can be very damaging to the ability of the University and the Patterson Institute when seeking funding from outside sources for our important programs. Although David seems untroubled, I am not sure why that is. We are all aware of his less than traditional marriage, but to date, that has never been an issue in funding. When one of his outside relationships erupt, as this one apparently has, there is cause for concern as it may have financial implications to the institutions we value.

I urge you to get your ship in order and do what is necessary to calm down whatever situation may exist.

As you know, I will be moving to Europe for an anticipated period of three to five years to attend to family business matters on the continent. I will, however, keep informed of the well being of the Patterson Institute, the Public Policy School, and the University. I anticipate your attention to this matter and that the less-than-optimal situation at the Public Policy School will be resolved in the near future. I do not mean to meddle, and your actions are your own, but I thought you should be aware that this family squabble has gotten out into the public at large.

Very Truly Yours,

Gregory Patterson, Jr.
Chairman
Board of Directors
The Patterson Institute

Exhibit 15

NITA UNIVERSITY

356 University Drive Nita City, Nita 69999

School of Public Policy Office of the Dean
Christine Jefferson, Ph.D., Dean

June 15, YR-2

Mary Anne Williams
Associate Professor
Nita University
School of Public Policy
Nita City, Nita 99999

Dear Professor Williams:

It is with regret that I must inform you that in my independent role as the Dean of the School of Public Policy I am unable to give a positive recommendation on your tenure to the University Board of Trustees as I do not believe a positive recommendation on your tenure would be in the long-term best interests of the University. As such, your tenure is denied. Unfortunately, this decision is a final one, and pursuant to University regulations, may not be reconsidered or reviewed. The reasons for my decision are multiple.

First, with regard to your teaching, scholarship and service, I agree with the dissent of Professor Binder as stated in your Tenure Review Report of May 5, YR-2. I do not believe that your low teaching evaluations in the very semester in which you applied for tenure is consistent with a finding of outstanding performance. I also do not believe that your scholarly production, although perhaps meeting minimal standards in quantity is sufficiently regular to show a continuing commitment to scholarship at an outstanding level. As you know, I was unable, pursuant to University regulations, to consider the unfinished article on which you are currently working. With regard to service, although your Committee work was acceptable, I share Professor Binder's trepidation about your inability to attract independent funding to the University.

All of that being said, your case would have been a close one, but for my opinion that you have demonstrated a severe lack of collegiality at both the University level as noted in your YR-5 Yearly Report of which you have a copy, and most recently in the School of Public Policy. It is axiomatic that collegiality is necessary for the effective operation of the School. We need not agree, but we must be civil and respectful. As you know, despite advice to the contrary, you have made numerous comments of the most negative sort regarding the academic and personal integrity of a senior member of the School of Public Policy Faculty that have been noted by individuals both within and without the University community. I have determined that such lack of collegiality is not in the long term best interests of the University.

Pursuant to University regulations I have decided to offer to you the opportunity to remain on the faculty of the School of Public Policy for the Fall YR-2 semester, after which your employment with the University is terminated.

I will be happy to discuss this most difficult decision with you, but as I have previously stated, my decision may not be reconsidered or reviewed.

Sincerely:

Christine Jefferson

Christine Jefferson, Ph.D.
Dean

cc: Margaret Dowling, Secretary
Nita University Board of Trustees

Howard Denberg, President
Nita University

Marvin Taylor, Ph.D.
Chair of the Tenurial Faculty
School of Public Policy

Tenurial Faculty
School of Public Policy

Exhibit 16

NITA UNIVERSITY

356 University Drive Nita City, Nita 69999

School of Public Policy

Mary Anne Williams, Ph.D., Associate Professor

June 30, YR-2

Christine Jefferson, Ph.D., Dean
Nita University
School of Public Policy
Nita City, Nita

Via: Campus Mail

Dear Dean Jefferson:

As you know from our recent conversation I am extremely upset and hurt by what I consider to be your unfair and wrong-minded decision to veto the vote of the tenurial faculty and not recommend my tenure to the University Board of Trustees. I can only assume that you have taken this extraordinary step, one that I understand is unprecedented in the School of Public Policy, to do the bidding of David Simonson. I had hoped that you would have had the integrity to stand up to him and his enormous bruised male ego, but it is well known among your colleagues that you are merely his stalking horse. Be aware that I intend to pursue every recourse regarding this matter available to me.

I decline to remain on the teaching faculty for the Fall YR-2 semester. You have made it untenable for me to have to face my colleagues and students because of your actions. I therefore request an unpaid leave of absence for the Fall YR-2 semester so that I may continue my health benefits until I can find suitable other employment.

It is my intention to return to my family home in the near future. You may send any correspondence to me at 85 Farm Hill Road, Wallingford, Conwell.

Sincerely,

Mary Anne Williams

Mary Anne Williams, Ph.D.
Associate Professor

Exhibit 17

TWIGGS, BATES & STRICKER, PC

ONE CONSTITUTION PLAZA
CONWELL CITY, CONWELL

July 6, YR-2

Ms. Terry Mattoon
NEEOC Complaints Investigator
Nita Equal Employment Opportunity Commission
1717 Spring Garden Street
Nita City, Nita 99998

Dear Ms. Mattoon:

Than you for speaking with me today on the phone regarding the claim of my client, Ms. Mary Anne Williams. Pursuant to your direction I am writing this letter by way of formal complaint regarding what I believe to be discriminatory behavior based on gender regarding her termination from employment by Nita University.

In its broadest terms, Ms. Williams claims that she was denied tenure, a designation she was qualified for and entitled to pursuant to the regulations of Nita University due to the discriminatory conduct of the University, through its agents, Christine Jefferson and David Simonson, among others to be determined at a later time. It is our claim that Ms. Williams was denied tenure in retaliation for her terminating a sexual relationship with David Simonson who was her supervisor at the Patterson Institute for Public Policy of Nita University and a chaired professor in the School of Public Policy. It is further claimed that Christine Jefferson, Ms. Williams supervisor at the Nita University School of Public Policy, conspired with David Simonson and used her authority as Dean to veto Ms. Williams's tenure in retaliation for Ms. Williams's termination of her sexual relationship with David Simonson. Finally, it is claimed that Nita University allowed a work environment hostile to women in general and Ms. Williams in particular to exist at the School of Public Policy to the employment detriment of Ms. Williams.

We will, of course, cooperate in any way that will be helpful to you in your inquiry. Thank you for your attention to this important matter.

Sincerely,

Charles R. Twiggs

Charles R. Twiggs
Attorney at Law

Exhibit 18

NITA UNIVERSITY
356 University Drive Nita City, Nita 69999

Date: July 8, YR-2

To: Nita University
Committee on Discrimination

From: Mary Anne Williams, Ph.D.
Associate Professor
School of Public Policy

Re: Discrimination Complaint

Attached please find a copy of a letter from my lawyer, Charles R. Twiggs, to the Nita Equal Employment Opportunity Commission.

For the reasons set forth in the attached letter I formally complain to this committee regarding the acts of discrimination described therein and ask that a full investigation be conducted and appropriate remedial action be taken, including, but not limited to, reinstatement on the faculty of the School of Public Policy with tenure at the rank of Associate Professor.

Any correspondence to me should be addressed and directed to my attorney.

Attachment

cc: Charles R. Twiggs
Attorney at Law

Exhibit 19

NITA UNIVERSITY

356 University Drive Nita City, Nita 69999

School of Public Policy

Mary Anne Williams, Ph.D., Associate Professor

February 12, YR-5

To: Nita University
Committee on Discrimination

From: Mary Anne Williams, Ph. D.
Assistant Professor
School of Public Policy

Re: Discrimination Complaint

I am writing to report and complain about offensive and inappropriate behavior of which I have been the target by Dean Richard Dressler of the Nita University Business School. For the past year I have served on the University Fund Raising Committee of which Dean Dressler is the Chair.

In that capacity I have been present at numerous social/fund raising gatherings where Dean Dressler was also present. On numerous occasions he has engaged in the following conduct all of which was unwarranted and offensive to me:

1. Suggested sexual contact and a sexual liaison;
2. Touched me inappropriately on my shoulder, waist, buttocks, and breasts;
3. Suggested sharing a room while on University business; and
4. Made numerous sexually suggestive and inappropriate comments about my appearance and otherwise.

Despite my making it clear that I was not interested in his advances and offended by his touching and his comments, his conduct has persisted and left me no resort other than this Committee.

Please understand that I do not make the complaint lightly. My only desire is to be free from this conduct as I find it extremely offensive and upsetting and it interferes with my ability to effectively perform my duties as a member of the University faculty.

Exhibit 20

NITA UNIVERSITY

356 University Drive Nita City, Nita 69999

School of Public Policy

RICHARD DRESSLER IS A GREAT MAN!!!!

LEAVE HIM ALONE. YOU ARE DRIVING HIM OUT OF THE UNIVERSITY.

REMEMBER—WHAT GOES AROUND, COMES AROUND!!!!!!!!!!!

Exhibit 21

NITA UNIVERSITY

356 University Drive Nita City, Nita 69999

School of Public Policy

***I HOPE* YOU ARE PROUD OF YOURSELF.**

A GOOD AND GREAT MAN IS GONE FROM HERE AND ALL BECAUSE OF *YOU*.

THERE ARE NO FREE LUNCHES.

YOU'LL REGRET THIS !!!!!

YOUR TIME WILL COME!!!!

Exhibit 22

NITA UNIVERSITY
356 University Drive Nita City, Nita 69999

School of Public Policy Office of the Dean
Christine Jefferson, Ph.D., Dean

November 22, YR-2

Dean Robert Verdana
Columbus University of Conwell
School of Public Policy
1400 W. Foundation Way
Conwell City, Conwell 77777

Dear Dean Verdana:

I am responding to you inquiry regarding Dr. Mary Anne Williams who, as I understand, is seeking an appointment on your faculty. Dr. Williams was a member of our faculty from YR-8 until YR-2 and because I have been the Dean of our School for that entire period I feel comfortable in offering to you my comments on her candidacy.

Dr. Williams came to be regarded as a very good teacher on our faculty. Her teaching evaluations rose during the course of her time at the School to more than acceptable levels, until unfortunately, the Spring YR-2 semester, when there was a significant downturn. I say it was unfortunate because, despite advice to the contrary, Dr. Williams chose to go forward on her tenure request in that very same semester.

With regard to scholarship, Dr. Williams produced two articles during her time with us. The first article in the Nita State University Journal of Public Policy was a first rate descriptive piece regarding unequal funding for inner city schools. Her second article, published in the Conwell University Journal of Contemporary Public Problems, a journal I believe you edited while on that faculty, was excellent in its content and execution. I believe that Dr. Williams has published another article since leaving us. Again unfortunately, she missed a deadline on that piece scheduled for publication in a symposium of the American Public Policy Review in Spring YR-2 and according to our regulations, that unfinished article was not available for our consideration on her tenure request.

Regarding service, Dr. Williams performed well on University and school committees and served as our faculty representative on the faculty senate. Her work at The Patterson Institute for Public Policy can best be described by David Simonson who I understand you have contacted. I do know, with regard to that work, that she was helpful in working on and obtaining of renewals of several grants. I am sure that Dr. Williams has informed you that she was denied tenure here because I determined that her tenure was not in the long-term best interests of the University despite a close positive vote by my faculty. This was a difficult decision for me but one that I thought necessary under the circumstances in which I found myself. I will leave to Dr. Williams to characterize my decision if you wish to pursue it with her as you may determine that those circumstances are not likely to repeat themselves and are of no moment to you.

In closing let me say that I believe that Dr. Williams has the intelligence, teaching talent and scholarly acumen to be a successful and productive member of a Public Policy School faculty. Although things did not work out for her at Nita University, I wish her well and good success in her future endeavors and perhaps she will be a good fit for your fine institution.

Warm regards to you, your family and my many friends on your faculty.

Sincerely,

Christine Jefferson

Christine Jefferson, Ph.D.,
Dean

Exhibit 23

PIPP

The Patterson Institute for Public Policy

Nita University
Nita City, Nita

David A. Simonson, Ph.D., Director

November 20, YR-2

Dean Robert Verdana
Columbus University of Conwell
School of Public Policy
1400 W. Foundation Way
Conwell City, Conwell 77777

Dear Dean Verdana:

I am in receipt of your letter seeking information regarding Dr. Mary Anne Williams who has applied for a teaching position with your fine school. As you know, Dr. Williams worked as a Researcher at the Patterson Institute for Public Policy under my direction for several years and although my opportunities to work with her were limited for the most part to one of our grants, I feel able to provide you with some information which you may find helpful in your decision making.

Dr. Williams's work as a Researcher was competent and resulted in acceptable work product on the reports and publications of the Patterson Institute. Her work on a major grant that I obtained from the U.S. Department of Education regarding Privatization of Public Schools was successful and of assistance in obtaining renewals of that grant. Dr. Williams's research was complete, her data compilation accurate and her written reports clear and concise. I would view her work at the Institute overall, as well within the acceptable range of professional activity and I am sure that she could replicate that work at CU.

In addition, Dr. Williams was a member of the Public Policy School faculty where she obtained a promotion from Assistant Professor to Associate Professor in normal course, but was unfortunately not recommended to the University for tenure. That fact should not, however, detract from her predominantly fine teaching evaluations and the publication of two significant articles of acceptable quality in her time on the faculty. She most definitely has the intellectual capacity to teach and produce scholarship at the level one would expect of a University professor.

In closing, let me say that I am sure that a decision to offer a position to Dr. Williams on your fine faculty would be a good one with numerous benefits to the CU Public Policy School and its many constituents.

If I can be of further assistance please feel free to call or write.

Sincerely,

David A. Simonson, Ph.D.
Director
Patterson Professor of Public Policy

Exhibit 24

NITA UNIVERSITY

356 University Drive Nita City, Nita 69999

School of Public Policy
Marvin Taylor, Ph.D., Beecher Professor of Public Policy

September 15, YR-2

Dean Robert Verdana
Columbus University of Conwell
School of Public Policy
1400 Foundation Way
Conwell City, Conwell 77777

Dear Bob:

I am writing to you on behalf of Professor Mary Anne Williams who has applied to your terrific school in response to the opening you have advertised in the recent edition of the Society of American Universities Newsletter. In my opinion she is an extraordinary talent and would be a great catch for your school.

Professor Williams served on our faculty for six years and attained a distinguished reputation as both a teacher and a scholar. In addition she did some excellent work at our Patterson Institute for Public Policy, where, according to David Simonson, Director and her supervisor, she was instrumental in obtaining renewals of a DOE grant in an area of her academic expertise, privatization of public schools, in the annual amount of $450,000.

As a teacher Professor Williams was current, coherent, and challenging for her students. She was evaluated by both students and faculty alike at a very high level. She inspired her best students, many of whom have gone on to graduate school in public policy, while at the same time leaving no student behind in achieving the best of which they were capable. As you are well aware, the mark of a great teacher is not the performance of the best students, but the worst. I have personally viewed her classes and found her to be engaging, articulate and always informative. You would be pleased and impressed with her classroom performance.

Professor Williams's scholarship is there for your perusal. Her first article with Nita State was an excellent first piece that is frequently cited in the literature. Her second article in your old journal, *CJCCP*, has received universal high marks throughout the profession. The fact that a relatively young academic was even published in *CJCCP*, is as you know, quite an accomplishment, but this piece more than held its own in the company of the high quality articles with which it shared an issue. And finally, her recent article in the *American Public Policy Review* which I know has been sent to you, will, in my opinion become known as the seminal piece on private school privatization. Any institution would be enhanced by having a scholar of Professor Williams's quality on its faculty.

I know that Professor Williams has been frank with you regarding her failure to receive tenure at Nita University. While I will be happy to discuss this with you privately, let it suffice to say that Christine Jefferson's veto of the faculty will on this issue was nothing less than a professional travesty.

In closing, I encourage you to carefully consider Professor Williams's candidacy. Meet with her; talk with her; I am sure you will be as impressed as I am.

If I can be of further assistance please call. It would be good to catch up on all your good works in any event.

Best wishes and warm regards from Howard and myself.

Sincerely,

Marvin Taylor, Ph.D.
Beecher Professor of Public Policy

Exhibit 25

NITA UNIVERSITY

356 University Drive Nita City, Nita 69999

School of Public Policy

Marvin Taylor, Ph.D., Beecher Professor of Public Policy

April 20, YR-1

Dr. Rose Clemmons
Director
The Beecher Institute
Freedom Place, Suite 12000
Nita City, Nita 99998

Dear Rose:

I am writing to suggest a Senior Researcher for the Beecher Institute. One of my former colleagues at the Public Policy School, Dr. Mary Anne Williams, is applying to a number of think tanks throughout the country and while I am sure she will have many offers, I have encouraged her to write to and speak with you about a position.

Mary Anne is a personal friend and was one of my favorite and most talented young faculty members at the School until she unfortunately feel victim to some nasty faculty politics at the hands of Christine Jefferson, who, despite a positive vote on tenure by the faculty, refused to recommend Mary Anne for tenure. It was a tremendous loss to our faculty, but may turn out to present an extraordinary opportunity for you and the Institute.

I have enclosed Mary Anne's resume for your consideration as well as copies of her articles and her grant reports referred to on that resume. I am sure you will be favorably impressed. Mary Anne has the researcher's tenacity, the reformer's intellect and the writer's communicative ability to meet your high standards. In addition, her excellent teaching skills will stand her in good stead in the presenting of testimony before the many legislative bodies that seek comment from the Institute.

I encourage you to recruit Mary Anne to your staff. She will make a great addition to the already talented group in your shop.

Warm regards from both Howard and myself.

Sincerely,

Marvin Taylor

Marvin Taylor, Ph.D.
Beecher Professor of Public Policy

Enclosure

Exhibit 26

PIPP

The Patterson Institute for Public Policy

Nita University
Nita City, Nita

David A. Simonson, Ph.D., Director

May 5, YR-1

Dr. Rose Clemmons
Director
The Beecher Institute
Freedom Place
Suite 12000
Nita City, Nita 99998

Dear Rose:

Thank you for your call today requesting a recommendation for Dr. Mary Anne Williams for a position on the professional staff of the Beecher Institute. During her time at the Patterson Institute I had many opportunities to work with and observe Dr. Williams in a professional setting and feel well qualified to provide you a positive recommendation for her filling the position you have open.

Dr. Williams worked on many of the projects of the Patterson Institute, but perhaps her most distinguished work was on a DOE grant regarding Privatization of Public Schools which generated a great deal of positive response for us as well as significant funding, and resulted in several renewals on which Dr. Williams took the laboring oar in drafting and preparing those proposals. Her work on that grant and other projects was uniformly well regarded, and her professionalism well regarded.

Although teaching is not a primary concern at Beecher, Dr. Williams was highly evaluated by both her students and her colleagues. More pertinent, her scholarship was well received in professional circles and her article in the *American Public Policy Review*, that was published this past October, accurately reflected the thinking and creativity that Dr. Williams brought to the Patterson Institute on the aforementioned public school privatization project. As you know, Professor Williams, although voted tenure by the faculty, did not receive a tenured position at Nita University. I do not believe that should be of any concern to you as tenure, in this day and age, more often reflects the economics of running a University and its long term plans, as much, or more, than the qualifications of the candidate.

In closing, let me say that I am sure that a decision to hire Dr. Williams will produce many long-term, positive effects for the Beecher Institute. She will bring intelligence, wisdom and enormous energy to your fine projects and the important work that the Beecher Institute has been associated with for many decades.

Thanks for the opportunity to recommend Dr. Williams. She will do a fine job for you.

Sincerely,

David A. Simonson, Ph.D.
Director
Patterson Professor of Public Policy
Nita University

Exhibit 27

The Beecher Institute Freedom Place Suite 12000 Nita City, Nita

May 15, YR-1

Dr. Mary Anne Williams
85 Farm Hill Road
Wallingford, Conwell 77744

Dear Dr. Williams:

It was a pleasure meeting with you several weeks ago. I am sorry that it took so long to get back to you but I have what I hope you will find to be some wonderful news. I have been authorized to offer you a position as a Senior Researcher at the Beecher Institute effective July 1, YR-1.

Your duties will include researching issues of public importance, preparing position papers, participating in symposia sponsored by the Institute, testifying before governmental bodies in support of Institute positions and participating in the ongoing effort of obtaining outside funding for the Institute's deserving projects. The position carries with it a beginning salary of $45,000 per year together with a benefits packages including health and retirement benefits as described in our benefits brochure and valued at 18 percent of salary.

Your contract will run year to year and you will be eligible for salary increases with each new contract.

If you agree to this offer please show the same by signing, dating, and returning one copy of this letter.

We are excited by the prospect of your joining our family.

Warm regards,

Rose Clemmons

Rose Clemmons, Ph.D.
Director

Mary Anne Williams

Mary Anne Williams

Date: May 17, YR-1

Exhibit 28

January 11, YR-0

To: *Williams v. Simonson*, et al.

Re: **Denise Morris, Ph.D.—Expert Economic Witness for the Defense**

The following information has been gleaned from answers to discovery, mandatory disclosures, and Dr. Morris's resume, and is available to both parties.

Dr. Denise Morris is fifty-two years old and the Chair of the Economics Department at Nita University. Her undergraduate degree is in Economics from the Wharton School of the University of Pennsylvania. She obtained her Ph.D. in Economics twenty-five years ago from the University of Pennsylvania, and has been employed as a member of the faculty of Nita University ever since. Professor Morris received tenure within five years of joining the faculty, which was two years before the norm, and was promoted to full Professor two years later, which was four years before the norm. Ten years ago she was named the Charles and Emily Burkett Professor of Economics, the most prestigious Chair within the Economics Department of the University. She has been Chair of the Economics Department for the past eight years. For a period of four years, ending at the end of the previous Presidential Administration, she served as a member of the Presidents Council on Economics, a blue ribbon panel that advised the President of the United States on economic matters.

Dr. Morris has written over one hundred books and articles in the field of economics. Most of her publications deal with international economic theory. She has, however, authored a general treatise entitled Forensic Economics that deals with the study of economic analysis as a tool for evaluating economic data in support of litigation. This volume was originally published fifteen years ago by Nita University Press. It is generally considered the standard text on forensic economics, covering many topics including evaluating economic loss for purposes of assessing damages in civil litigation. Her book, in its latest edition published last year, contains a chapter on economic valuation of hedonic damages in which she lays out the various theoretical models for evaluating such non-economic claims as the loss of joys of life as the result of physical or emotional injury. Professor Morris takes the position that the use of an economic model to attempt to evaluate hedonic damages is not yet refined enough to be considered reliable for use in litigation. The book is currently in its seventh edition and is used as a text in over a hundred and fifty universities around the world. Even though this book is well-recognized, Dr. Morris views the study of forensic economics as an academic sideline to her main interest in international economics.

Dr. Morris does not regularly testify as an expert witness in support of litigation. In the past four years she appeared in a deposition and later at trial in only one case where a member of the university community was severely injured in an automobile accident. The trial testimony occurred two years ago. In that case, her report contained an economic valuation of the loss of the joys of life (hedonic damages) of the injured plaintiff due to her injuries. Her testimony on this topic was not admitted by the trial judge who made a finding that the theory on which that opinion was based was not generally accepted in the field of economics, had not been the subject of peer review, had not been tested for accuracy and was therefore not sufficiently reliable to be helpful to the jury. In a footnote in her treatise chapter on evaluation of hedonic damages, Professor Morris admits to having taken the position she did in the litigation described above and then goes on to explain why by the time of the writing of her chapter she decided that at least for the time-being, and until further research and study could be accomplished, to reject the calculation of hedonic damages as a reliable economic theory.

Professor Morris's new edition of her Forensic Economics treatise has been published and there have been, to date, five responsive articles in respected economic journals that have considered the theories she describes regarding economic assessment of hedonic damages. Three of those articles, all by well regarded economists, agree with her conclusion that the methods described for such calculations are still unreliable and amount to nothing more than educated guess work, and that the assumptions made in order to perform the calculation of these damages do not have an adequate economic predicate. The other two articles, also in respected journals and by respected economists, take the position that accurate evaluation of hedonic damages is a viable and useful economic theory. To date, there is no court in the State of Nita that has allowed expert economist testimony on the valuation of hedonic damages, although such testimony has been recognized in some federal courts around the country. See *Sherrod v. Berry*, U.S. Court of Appeals for the 7th Circuit, 1984.

Professor Morris claims no particular expertise regarding the employment of people who hold Ph.D. degrees in Public Policy. She views these professionals as members of the service sector of the economy, providing expertise to academics, governmental agencies, legislative bodies, political think-tanks, and in the private sector, for entities seeking to influence public policy.

To date, Professor Morris has charged the Defendants $5,000 for the economic analysis she performed, consultation with counsel, and the preparation of her report.

Professor Morris does not know any of the parties well. She has met Professor Simonson on one occasion and has served on several university committees with Dean Jefferson. She has not socialized with either of them. She has never met Mary Anne Williams.

Dr. Morris was a Professor in the School of Economics when Brian Sullivan, the expert witness for the Plaintiff was a graduate student. She, of course, knew Dr. Sullivan as a student, as at any given time there are less than thirty Ph.D. candidates in residence in the Economics Department at the University, but did not supervise any of his work. She recalls him as a good, if not brilliant student. She is aware of his business, The Nita Center for Forensic Economics, and regards that group as a necessary evil in modern litigious society. She has written an article decrying such organizations for their lack of economic principals, fashioning, as some such organizations do, opinions based on the exigencies of the case, changing theoretical models to suit each client of the firm. She has not actually reviewed any of the Center's or Sullivan's work, except with regard to this case.

Five years ago Dr. Morris and the Nita University Economics Department received a grant from the Patterson Foundation (which also provided the seed grant for the Defendant Patterson Institute) in the amount of $750,000 to study the economics of the effect of patent protection on prescription drugs on emerging economic systems. Dr. Morris was a signatory on the grant application as Chair of the Economics Department, but was not the Principal Investigator and has not profited personally from the grant. She will concede that the grant was a major one for the Economics Department and that she hopes to obtain funding in the future from the Patterson Foundation.

Exhibit 29

January 25, YR-0

To: *Williams v. Simonson*

Re: **Brian Sullivan, Ph.D.—Expert economic witness for the Plaintiff**

The following information has been gleaned from answers to discovery, mandatory disclosures, and the resume of Dr. Sullivan. This information is available to both parties.

Dr. Sullivan is forty years old. He obtained his undergraduate degree with honors from the University of North Carolina in economics. He received his Ph.D. degree in economics from the University of Nita (with honors) fifteen years ago. Dr. Sullivan worked for five years as an economist at the Beecher Institute, which is a political think-tank in Nita City, and coincidentally, the Plaintiff's current employer. Ten years ago he began his own consulting business—the Nita Center for Forensic Economics. Dr. Sullivan is the owner of that firm and currently employs ten other economists and twenty other support employees in his Nita City offices. The business of the Center for Forensic Economics is to provide litigation support in performing economic analyses regarding items of claimed economic damage.

Dr. Sullivan appears on a regular basis as an expert witness in depositions and trials. In many other engagements he has provided reports regarding economic analysis in matters where there was a settlement reached between the parties. In the past four years he has testified in an average of eighteen depositions per year and ten trials per year. His testimony has been exclusively for plaintiffs in personal injury and employment cases, although there are economists in his firm who testify frequently for defendants in such cases. Dr. Sullivan has had at least fifteen engagements involving claims of discrimination against university-level faculty members, including one case five years ago against Nita University for a professor who was denied tenure in the English department. He was also engaged as an expert witness by the counsel for Professor Lydia Greenfield approximately eight years ago in a potential gender discrimination claim against Nita University and the School of Public Policy involving an allegation against Professor Simonson. Both of those cases settled after Dr. Sullivan completed his analysis and report, but without protracted litigation and without Dr. Sullivan providing any deposition testimony.

Dr. Sullivan has been qualified as an expert witness in the field of economics over a hundred times and no court has failed to recognize him as a qualified expert economist. In the past ten years he has had no publications. He has, however, been a frequent speaker before state and local bar associations and for ATLA conferences around the country on issues of forensic economics.

Dr. Sullivan's average fee for each case in which he appears is between $7,500 and $10,000, including the time spent in performing his economic analysis, consulting with counsel, preparation of his report and time spent in deposition and trial testimony. His annual billings are in the range of $240,000. To date, Dr. Sullivan has been paid $7,000 for his time in conducting his economic analysis, consulting with counsel, and preparing his report and a response to the report of Dr. Morris in this case.

Dr. Sullivan has been retained by Plaintiff's law firm (Twiggs, Bates & Stricker) in five previous cases, all occurring in the past two years.

Dr. Sullivan was a Ph.D. student at the University of Nita while Professor Morris (Defendant's expert economist) was on the faculty. He did not take any of her courses, nor did she supervise his work as Professor Morris's expertise was predominantly in international economics which was not Dr. Sullivan's area of interest.

Dr. Sullivan recognizes Dr. Morris's treatise, *Forensic Economics* as an authoritative text in the field, but he did not rely on it in performing his economic analysis in this case. The first edition of this book, now in its seventh edition, was not published until the year that Dr. Sullivan received his Ph.D. so he did not use it in his course work. He notes that although Dr. Morris does not specialize in forensic economics, her book is an excellent compilation of the basics of the field. He specifically states that he does not agree with the conclusions espoused by Dr. Morris in the most recent edition of her book regarding the economic evaluation of hedonic damages as stated in his report. Dr. Sullivan has admitted in a deposition in another of his cases that a senior economist in his firm, who works predominantly for defendants in cases such as this one, has written reports rejecting as invalid the purported economic analysis of hedonic damages, using Dr. Morris's work as a predicate for his opinion. Dr. Sullivan stated specifically in that deposition that he does not agree with Dr. Morris's conclusions and does believe such economic analysis (of hedonic damages) is valid.

Although Dr. Sullivan has never been permitted to testify regarding his economic analysis of hedonic damages in a court in the State of Nita, he has given such testimony on one occasion in a federal court in the neighboring State of Conwell. There was no legal precedent set in that case because the case was settled before closing arguments and there were no appeals taken. He admits that most courts have ruled that the economic analysis of hedonic damages does not pass *Daubert/Kumho* Tire muster. He has stated in recent depositions in other cases, however, that the economic theory supporting calculation of hedonic damages is receiving greater acceptance in the economic community and that he feels that within a short period of time, if not already, that the theories supporting such calculations will become generally accepted as valid.

Exhibit 30

NITA UNIVERSITY
356 University Drive Nita City, Nita 69999

Department of Economics
Patterson Building

March 29, YR-0

Meredith Aquino, Esquire
Flywheel, Shyster, and Flywheel
One Gilded Corporate Tower
Penthouse Suite
Nita City, NT 69999

Re: *Mary Anne Williams v. David Simonson, et al.*
Our File Number: 8675309
From: Denise Morris, Ph.D.

Dear Ms. Aquino:

The following is our analysis of the economic loss in the above-captioned matter. We reserve the right to revise or supplement this report based upon the receipt of additional information.

Documents Reviewed

The following documents in the above-captioned matter have been reviewed:

- Complaint and Exhibits 1–27
- Answer and Counterclaim of Defendant Simonson
- Deposition transcript of Mary Anne Williams, Marvin Taylor, David Simonson, and Christine Jefferson
- Assessment of Economic Loss authored by the Nita Center for Forensic Economics

In addition to the foregoing, I have relied upon various professional and governmental publications as are more fully cited herein.

Introduction

Mary Anne Williams is a 32-year-old Ph.D. that currently works as senior researcher at the Beecher Institute here in Nita City. Ms. Williams also teaches classes at Nita Community College.

From June of YR-8 until May of YR-2 Ms. Williams taught at Nita University's School of Public Policy. During much of this time she was also employed as a researcher at the Patterson Institute of Public Policy which has personal and business ties to Nita University.

On October 12, YR-3, Ms. Williams was offered the position of Associate Director of the Patterson Institute starting on July 1, YR-2. The offer was conditioned on Ms. Williams receiving tenure in May YR-2. The offer letter was authored by the director of the Patterson Institute, David Simonson who was, at the time, having an affair with Ms. Williams.

During the Spring semester of YR-2, Ms. Williams' personal problems affected her classroom performance as well as her relationship with other faculty members in the Public Policy Department. In addition, she missed a publication deadline for *The American Public Policy Review*. As a result, she was denied tenure by her department in May of YR-2. Following the tenure decision, Ms. Williams was offered employment through the end of YR-2 to give her time to find another position but she decided to take a leave of absence without pay instead.

Recent Earning History

Ms. Williams' salary for her last year at Nita University was $70,000. She was also receiving a stipend from the Patterson Institute of $11,500 for research she was performing for Dr. Simonson. As a senior researcher for the Beecher Institute, Ms. Williams' salary, starting on July 1, YR-1 was $46,000.

Analysis of Economic Loss

It should be noted that any calculation of economic loss assumes that Ms. Williams' failure to achieve tenure was based on discriminatory actions by the Defendants as described in the Complaint.

Potential Earnings as a tenured professor

Ms. Williams' salary as an associate professor at Nita University was $70,000. It has been represented that the average salary for a full professor with tenure at Nita University is $105,000. It should be noted, however, that the highest paid professors at the University are in the school of Business and Finance.[1] Furthermore, the average full professor at Nita University is 52 years.

The average salary among tenured professors in the school of public policy is $95,000. Most of these professors supplement their salaries via publishing and consulting. It was assumed that Ms. Williams' projected salary would increase to $95,000 in YR+20, or her age 52. In addition to her University salary, it was assumed that Ms. Williams would continue to earn $11,500 per year in consulting fees. I recognize that Dr. Simonson had offered her a more lucrative position at the Patterson Institute but,

[1] This fact is attributable to market forces. To attract quality staff in this department, the University must compete with large corporations in the private sector. The result being that this department has the highest per professor salaries in the University.

in my opinion, given their personal relationship, this position was not likely to materialize.[2] Earnings projections begin on January 1, YR-1.

Present Value

Future earnings are reduced to present value in recognition that the Plaintiff will receive future compensation in the current year. I have used a net discount rate of 2 percent which is consistent recent economic history, federal law and Nita State Court guidelines.

Earnings after January 1, YR-1

In her statement, Ms. Williams' said she sent out a hundred resumes the result of which were interviews with Nita State and an out of state university. Eventually she landed a research position with the Beecher Institute with a salary of $46,000. Ms. Williams has indicated that top researchers at Beecher earn $60,000. Ms. Williams also earns $7,500 a year as a part-time teacher at Nita Community College. I have employed these figures in calculating post-separation earnings for purposes of back pay.

Duration of Economic Loss

Drs. Staller and Sullivan have calculated the economic loss as the difference between full professor earnings at Nita University and earnings as a researcher at Beecher through Ms. Williams's age 67. In other words, Drs. Staller and Sullivan assume that for the next 35 years, Ms. Williams will continue to work in a job for which she is apparently overqualified and compensated at less than half of what she herself has said is the average for University professors.

What is more likely, in my opinion, is that Ms. Williams will continue to seek appropriate employment and will be successful in finding it within twelve months. This scenario is not based on an unfounded assumption. In her statement, Ms. Williams mentions another female professor in the school of public policy who left under similar circumstances in YR-8. It is clear from Dr. Taylor's statement that the professor is Lydia Greenfield. It is important to note that professor Greenfield secured a position with Nita State University and is currently a tenured full professor there.

We also note that Dr. Williams' article in The American Public Policy Review was published in October of YR-2. This accomplishment, along with her other credentials should be enough to secure another University position. Assuming a rigorous job search, it is anticipated that Ms. Williams could recapture her pre-separation earnings as early as 18 months, or by the end of YR+1 (approximately 20 months). It is my understanding that there is data published by the Bureau of Labor Statistics which supports a five year catch up. I doubt, however, that the average person has the resume of Ms. Williams. A second, more conservative measure of loss assumes that Ms. Williams' post-separation earnings will catch up to her projected earnings at Nita University within five years.

Alternatively, if Ms. Williams is no longer seeking employment commensurate with her former position at Nita University, I am advised by counsel that this could result in a bar to economic recovery.

[2] In fact, Plaintiff's economic consultants, Drs. Staller and Sullivan, recognized this fact by excluding the Patterson salary from one of their estimates of potential earnings.

Fringe Benefits

Ms. Williams current fringe benefits packages at Beecher and Nita Community College are substantially equivalent to those she enjoyed at Nita University. Therefore, we have not valued any loss from these benefits.

Hedonic Damages

Drs. Staller and Sullivan include additional damages calculations purported to value a diminution of life's pleasures to Ms. Williams. My search of the literature found that hedonic damages have only been presented in wrongful death cases or cases involving permanent personal injury (e.g., quadriplegia). Articles in the Journal of Forensic of Economics debunking hedonic damages far outnumber those that champion this dubious concept of damages. More importantly, testimony on hedonic damages has been rejected for lack of scientific foundation in the majority of jurisdictions where it has been presented.

In the matter of Ms. Williams, while she may have had a few difficult months following the tenure vote in YR-2, she has returned to teaching and apparently has a new (single) man in her life. To suggest that Ms. Williams has experienced a permanent diminution of life's pleasures is simply contrary to the facts.

Summary

As outlined in the attached table, the economic loss to Ms. Williams ranges from $140,109 to $172,182. Please do not hesitate to contact me if you have further questions.

Sincerely,

Denise Morris, Ph.D.

Denise Morris, Ph.D.
Chairman, Department of Economics
Nita University

DM/dra

Mary Anne Williams —Lost Earnings—				
YEAR	AGE	PRE-TERM	POST-TERM	NET LOSS
YR-2	30	35,000	—	35,000
YR-1	31	80,000	23,000	57,000
YR-0	32	81,500	54,773	26,727
YR+1	33	83,000	61,618	21,382
YR+2	34	84,500	68,464	16,036
YR+3	35	86,000	75,309	10,691
YR+4	36	87,500	82,155	5,345
YR+5	37	89,000	89,000	—
Total Back Pay Earnings				118,727
Front Pay to December 31, YR+1				21,382
Back Pay plus Front Pay to December 31, YR+1				140,109
Front Pay Earnings to YR+5				53,455
Back Pay Plus Front Pay to YR+5				172,182

Exhibit 31

NITA CENTER FOR FORENSIC ECONOMICS

1608 Walnut Street Eighth Floor Suite 888 Nita City, NT 69999
(555) 546-5600 Fax (555) 732-8158
nitaeconomics@nitanet.com www.cfes.com

Assessment of Economic Loss in the Matter of
Mary Anne Williams, Ph.D. v. David L. Simonson, et al.

This report has been prepared for the use of counsel in the instant matter. Any other transmission, copy, or utilization of this report or material contained herein is prohibited without the written consent of the Nita Center for Forensic Economics.

Prepared and Submitted by:

Jerome M. Staller, Ph.D.

Brian P. Sullivan, Ph.D.

March 1, YR-0

Assessment of Economic Loss
in the Matter of
Mary Anne Williams, Ph.D. v. David L. Simonson, et al.
March YR-0

I. INTRODUCTION AND BACKGROUND

This report assesses the economic loss suffered by Mary Anne Williams, Ph.D. as a result of employment discrimination that occurred in June of YR-2. The economic loss consists of lost earnings and fringe benefits.

Dr. Williams joined the faculty of the Nita University School of Public Policy as an Associate Professor in the fall of YR-8. In YR-6 Dr. Williams took an additional position as a researcher at the Patterson Institute of Public Policy. In June of YR-3, Dr. Williams was promoted to Assistant Professor. On October 12, YR-3, Dr. Williams was offered the position of Associate Director of the Patterson Institute. The position was to commence on July 1, YR-2 and was contingent on her receiving tenure at Nita University. Despite a favorable vote on tenure in May YR-2, Christine Jefferson, the Dean of Nita University's School of Public Policy, vetoed the decision and denied Dr. Williams' tenure. Dean Jefferson offered Dr. Williams a teaching position for the fall semester to give Dr. Williams time to find another position but she elected to take a leave of absence through the end of that year.

During her leave of absence, Dr. Williams sought counseling to combat feelings of depression. She was forced to sell her recently purchased Nita City condominium at a loss and move in with her parents.

Dr. Williams represents that she undertook a thorough employment search, sending out a hundred resumes to various universities. Due to defamatory letters of recommendation from faculty members at Nita University, she said, she was unable to find employment as a professor. In YR-1, she found a position as a senior researcher at Beecher Institute.

Dr. Williams is single and resides in Nita City. She is currently 32 years of age.

II. WORKLIFE AND LIFE EXPECTANCY

In calculating Dr. Williams' economic loss, we offer two worklife estimates. In our first estimate, it was assumed that the plaintiff would have been continuously employed to age 67. In our second estimate we adjust earnings to account for statistical worklife data.[1] According to *Worklife Estimates: Effects of Race and Education* (U.S. Department of Labor, Bureau of Labor Statistics, February, 1986), the average worklife expectancy for individuals with more than 15 years of education is to age 62.3, based on the plaintiff's current age of 32. We have employed this data in our statistical worklife tables.

[1] Statistical worklife is an allowance for periods of voluntary detachment or absence from the labor market for reasons such as sickness, educational advancement, or the probability of death.

III. PRE-TERMINATION EARNINGS—Earnings Absent the Discrimination

1. Base of Earnings

Dr. Williams' salary as an Associate Professor was $70,000 per year. The average salary of a tenured full professor at Nita University is $105,000. It was assumed, absent the discrimination, that Dr. Williams would have achieved this level of compensation after ten years of tenure in YR+9. Earnings from YR-2 to YR+9 were assumed to increase at a linear rate. As noted previously, Dr. Williams was offered the position of Assistant Director at the Patterson Institute. This position would have paid her $24,000 per year (in addition to her faculty salary at Nita University) starting on July 1, YR-2. As this position was contingent on making tenure, this salary represents potential additional lost earnings as a result of employment discrimination. We also note that this position was offered nine months prior to the start date and that the duration of the position was not specified. Therefore we have presented pre-termination earnings with and without the salary from the Patterson Institute position.

2. Discount Rate

Future earnings have been discounted to their present values by employing a net discount rate. To derive an appropriate real rate of discount, we examined the interest rates offered on High Grade Municipal Bonds and the average annual rate of change in the Employment Cost Index. Using data from the Economic Report of the President February YR-0, we have calculated a real discount rate of 1.5 percent.

IV. FRINGE BENEFITS

As a tenured professor, Dr. Williams' fringe benefits would include employer-paid health insurance (including prescription plan, vision, and dental coverage); a 401(k) savings and investment pension plan with employer match up to 6 percent of salary; a defined benefit pension plan; a $150,000 life insurance policy; a long term disability plan; paid sabbaticals; subsidized meals at the faculty cafeteria; access to the Nita University Credit Union; five weeks of paid vacation; attendance at up to three one-week public policy seminars held across the country; and free access to all of the campus athletic facilities (e.g., fitness center, squash courts, indoor pool, tennis courts, and running track). These employer paid benefits are estimated at 27 percent of salary.

V. POST TERMINATION EARNINGS

1. Base of Earnings

After an extensive job search, Dr. Williams secured a position as a Senior Researcher with the Beecher Institute in Nita City, starting on July 1, 2003. Dr. Beecher's initial salary was $46,000. It is assumed that her salary will increase to $60,000 after ten years, which is what the top earners at Beecher make. Dr. Williams has also taken a position as an adjunct professor at Nita Community College, earning $7,500 per year teaching evening courses.

2. Duration of Loss

As discussed in Claim VI of the Complaint, various defendants provided defamatory statements to prospective employers subsequent to Dr. Williams' termination. The net effect of Defendant's actions were that Dr. Williams post-termination earnings capacity may be permanently limited. That is, the difference between her earning capacity as a University Professor and her post-termination earning capacity may be a permanent artifact. This permanent, ongoing loss is shown in Tables One and Two.

Assuming that the defamation has not permanently impacted Dr. Williams' post-termination earning capacity, we have provided a second model of economic loss where post-termination earnings catch-up to her potential earnings as a University professor. The concept of an earnings catch up is supported by published statistics. The U.S. Department of Labor reports on a biannual survey of displaced workers. This Displaced Worker Survey is conducted in even numbered years by the Census Bureau for the Labor Department. Recent results of this survey are reported in *The Monthly Labor Review* (April 1995). This survey has been relied upon in academic literature dealing with the topic of worker displacement and readjustment to the labor market. For example, Adam Seitchik notes in "Who Are Displaced Workers?" *Job Displacement: Consequences and Implications for Policy* (J.T. Addison, ed.) that the Displaced Worker Survey has become the "industry standard" in this type of labor market research. Studies by J.T. Addison and P. Portugal, "Job Displacement, Relative Wage Changes, and Duration of Unemployment", *Journal of Labor Economics* (1989) and L. Kletzer, "Returns to Seniority After Permanent Job Loss," *American Economic Review* (June 1989) both support the catch up by displaced workers, especially those with transferable skills.

The survey data supports the concept that workers who are displaced from their previous employer can attain a complete catch up in earnings to the level which would have been paid by the separating employer after within ten years. Therefore, we have calculated lost earnings based on a catch-up of post-termination earnings by YR+10.

3. *Fringe Benefits*

As a part-time employee at Nita Community College, Dr. Williams does not receive fringe benefits from the college. As a full-time employee at Beecher Institute, Dr. Williams receives the following employer paid benefits: health insurance (no vision or dental), a 401(k) plan with a 50 percent employer match up to 6 percent of salary, two weeks of paid vacation (three weeks after five years). Fringe benefits from the Beecher Institute were estimated at 18 percent of salary.

VI. HEDONIC DAMAGES

1. *The Value of the Loss of Life's Pleasures*

Dr. Williams spent most of her adult life preparing to teach at the University level. Subsequent to her discriminatory treatment, she has suffered from bouts of depression, which have affected her personal and professional life. In other words, she has suffered a diminution of the value of life's pleasures. Economists have been asked to place a value on the loss of life's pleasures, or hedonic damages, for many years, and expert testimony on this point has been presented and accepted in jurisdictions across the U.S. Data useful for calculation of hedonic damages flow from two sources. First, several studies have examined consumer decisions with respect to safety enhancements in automobiles, purchase of smoke detectors, memberships in gyms and athletic clubs and purchase of home security systems. Detailed econometric studies have examined consumer spending on such items in light of the life-saving benefits offered. For example, if a smoke detector has a one out of 100,000 chance of saving a life and consumers purchase one million detectors at $25 each, the implicit valuation of life is $2.5 million.

The second source of data arises from "compensatory differential" studies of wage rates. For example, if the risk to a factory worker of a loss of life is one out of 10,000 while the risk to a retail worker is 1 out of 40,000 and 40,000 factory workers are paid 10 cents per hour more than retail workers, the compensating differential is $8 million (10 cents per hour multiplied by 2,000 hours multiplied by 40,000 workers) all divided by four lives saved (40, 000 * 1/10,000 - 40, 000 * 1/40,000). Miller has presented a review of thirty-five such studies in the *Journal of Forensic Economics* (1994). His range is from $6 and $10 million for a complete loss of life. Assuming a 20 percent diminution, the hedonic damages to Dr. Williams ranges from $1.2 to $2 million.

VII. TABLES

Table 1 shows lost back pay and front pay calculations including earnings from the Patterson Institute absent the discrimination. Table 2 shows lost back pay and front pay without earnings from the Patterson Institute absent the discrimination. Table 3 shows lost back pay and front pay calculations including earnings from the Patterson Institute absent the discrimination. Table 2 shows lost back pay and front pay without earnings from the Patterson Institute absent the discrimination. Tables 3 and 4 show back pay and front pay with a ten-year catch up of earnings with and without earnings from the Patterson Institute.

VIII. SUMMARY

As outlined in the Summary Tables below, Dr. Williams' total economic damages range from $1,387,649 to $2,301,464. Assuming that the effect of Defendant's defamation is not permanent, Dr. Williams' total economic damages range from $351,993 to $537,235.

Hedonic damages represent an additional $1.2 million to $2 million.

Mary Anne Williams—Summary Table*
Assuming Permanent Defamation

***Does not include hedonic damages**

	INCLUDING EARNINGS FROM PATTERSON	*EXCLUDING EARNINGS FROM PATTERSON*
Back Pay Earnings Loss	181,909	119,727
Fringe Benefits	40,676	40,676
Total Back Pay Loss	**222,585**	**160,403**
Front Pay Earnings to Statistical Worklife	1,383,521	722,040
Fringe Benefits	455,207	455,207
Total Front Pay to Statistical Worklife	**1,838,728**	**1,227,246**
Back Pay plus Front Pay to Statistical Worklife	2,061,313	1,387,649
Front Pay Earnings to Age 67	1,562,840	873,452
Fringe Benefits	516,038	516,038
Total Front Pay to Age 67	**2,078,879**	**1,389,491**
Back Pay plus Front Pay to Age 67	2,301,464	1,549,894

Mary Anne Williams—Summary Table*
Assuming A Ten-Year Catch Up

***Does not include hedonic damages**

	INCLUDING EARNINGS FROM PATTERSON	*EXCLUDING EARNINGS FROM PATTERSON*
Back Pay Earnings Loss	181,909	119,727
Fringe Benefits	40,676	40,676
Total Back Pay Loss	**222,585**	**160,403**
Front Pay Earnings	257,150	143,005
Fringe Benefits	57,500	48,584
Total Front Pay	**314,651**	**191,590**
Back Pay plus Front Pay	537,235	351,993

Table One—Mary Anne Williams, Ph.D. Economic Loss—Including earnings from Patterson				
YEAR	***AGE***	***PRE-TERM***	***POST-TERM***	***NET LOSS***
YR-2	30	47,000	—	47,000
YR-1	31	104,720	23,000	81,720
YR-0	32	107,962	54,773	53,189
YR+1	33	110,085	63,435	46,651
YR+2	34	112,215	64,707	47,507
YR+3	35	114,349	65,980	48,369
YR+4	36	116,490	67,253	49,237
YR+5	37	118,635	68,526	50,109
YR+6	38	120,786	69,798	50,987
YR+7	39	122,942	71,071	51,871
YR+8	40	125,103	72,344	52,759
YR+9	41	127,269	73,616	53,652
YR+10	42	125,388	74,889	65,388
YR+11	43	123,535	73,782	49,752
YR+12	44	121,709	72,692	49,017
YR+13	45	119,910	71,618	48,293
YR+14	46	118,138	70,559	47,579
YR+15	47	116,392	69,517	46,876
YR+16	48	114,672	68,489	46,183
YR+17	49	112,978	67,477	45,501
YR+18	50	111,308	66,480	44,828
YR+19	51	109,663	65,497	44,166
YR+20	52	108,042	64,530	43,513
YR+21	53	106,446	63,576	42,870
YR+22	54	104,873	62,636	42,236
YR+23	55	103,323	61,711	41,612
YR+24	56	101,796	60,799	40,997
YR+25	57	100,292	59,900	40,391
YR+26	58	98,809	59,015	39,794
YR+27	59	97,349	58,143	39,206
YR+28	60	95,911	57,284	38,627
YR+29	61	94,493	56,437	38,056
YR+30	62	93,097	55,603	37,494
YR+31	63	91,721	54,781	36,940
YR+32	64	90,365	53,972	36,394
YR+33	65	89,030	53,174	35,856
YR+34	66	87,714	52,388	35,326
YR+35	67	86,418	51,614	34,804

Back Pay Earnings Fringe Benefits	181,909 40,676
Total Back Pay Loss	222,585
Front Pay Earnings to Statistical Worklife	1,383,521
Fringe Benefits	455,207
Total Front Pay to Statistical Worklife	1,838,728
Back Pay plus Front Pay to Statistical Worklife	2,061,313
Front Pay Earnings to Age 67	1,562,840
Fringe Benefits	516,038
Total Front Pay to Age 67	2,078,879
Back Pay plus Front Pay to Age 67	2,301,464

Table Two—Mary Anne Williams, Ph.D. Economic Loss—Excluding earnings from Patterson				
YEAR	***AGE***	***PRE-TERM***	***POST-TERM***	***NET LOSS***
YR-2	30	35,000	—	35,000
YR-1	31	80,000	23,000	57,000
YR-0	32	82,500	54,773	27,727
YR+1	33	85,000	63,435	21,565
YR+2	34	87,500	64,707	22,793
YR+3	35	90,000	65,980	24,020
YR+4	36	92,500	67,253	25,247
YR+5	37	95,000	68,526	26,474
YR+6	38	97,500	69,798	27,702
YR+7	39	100,000	71,071	28,929
YR+8	40	102,500	72,344	30,156
YR+9	41	105,000	73,616	31,384
YR+10	42	103,448	74,889	43,448
YR+11	43	101,919	73,782	28,137
YR+12	44	100,413	72,692	27,721
YR+13	45	98,929	71,618	27,312
YR+14	46	97,467	70,559	26,908
YR+15	47	96,027	69,517	26,510
YR+16	48	94,608	68,489	26,119
YR+17	49	93,210	67,477	25,733
YR+18	50	91,832	66,480	25,352
YR+19	51	90,475	65,497	24,978
YR+20	52	89,138	64,530	24,608
YR+21	53	87,821	63,576	24,245
YR+22	54	86,523	62,636	23,886
YR+23	55	85,244	61,711	23,533
YR+24	56	83,984	60,799	23,186
YR+25	57	82,743	59,900	22,843
YR+26	58	81,520	59,015	22,505
YR+27	59	80,316	58,143	22,173
YR+28	60	79,129	57,284	21,845
YR+29	61	77,959	56,437	21,522
YR+30	62	76,807	55,603	21,204
YR+31	63	75,672	54,781	20,891
YR+32	64	74,554	53,972	20,582
YR+33	65	73,452	53,174	20,278
YR+34	66	72,367	52,388	19,978
YR+35	67	71,297	51,614	19,683

Back Pay Earnings Fringe Benefits	119,727 40,676
Total Back Pay Loss	160,403
Front Pay Earnings to Statistical Worklife	772,040
Fringe Benefits	455,207
Total Front Pay to Statistical Worklife	1,227,246
Back Pay plus Front Pay to Statistical Worklife	1,387,649
Front Pay Earnings to Age 67	873,452
Fringe Benefits	516,038
Total Front Pay to Age 67	1,389,491
Back Pay plus Front Pay to Age 67	1,549,894

Table Three—Mary Anne Williams, Ph.D. Economic Loss—Ten-Year Catch Up Including earnings from Patterson				
YEAR	***AGE***	***PRE-TERM***	***POST-TERM***	***NET LOSS***
YR-2	30	47,000	—	47,000
YR-1	31	104,720	23,000	81,720
YR-0	32	107,962	54,773	53,189
YR+1	33	110,085	61,834	48,251
YR+2	34	112,215	68,896	43,319
YR+3	35	114,349	75,957	38,392
YR+4	36	116,490	83,019	33,471
YR+5	37	118,635	90,080	28,555
YR+6	38	120,786	97,142	23,644
YR+7	39	122,942	104,203	18,738
YR+8	40	125,103	111,265	13,838
YR+9	41	127,269	118,326	8,942
YR+10	42	125,388	125,388	—
Back Pay Earnings Loss Fringe Benefits				181,909 40,676
Total Back Pay Loss				222,585
Front Pay Earnings Loss				257,150
Fringe Benefits				57,500
Total Front Pay Loss				314,651
Back Pay plus Front Pay				537,235

Table Four—Mary Anne Williams, Ph.D. Economic Loss—Ten-Year Catch Up Excluding earnings from Patterson				
YEAR	***AGE***	***PRE-TERM***	***POST-TERM***	***NET LOSS***
YR-2	30	35,000	—	35,000
YR-1	31	80,000	23,000	57,000
YR-0	32	82,500	54,773	27,727
YR+1	33	85,000	59,640	25,360
YR+2	34	87,500	64,508	22,992
YR+3	35	90,000	69,375	20,625
YR+4	36	92,500	74,243	18,257
YR+5	37	95,000	79,111	15,889
YR+6	38	97,500	83,978	13,522
YR+7	39	100,000	88,846	11,154
YR+8	40	102,500	93,713	8,787
YR+9	41	105,000	98,581	6,419
YR+10	42	103,448	103,448	—
Back Pay Earnings Loss Fringe Benefits				119,727 40,676
Total Back Pay Loss				160,403
Front Pay Earnings Loss				143,005
Fringe Benefits				48,584
Total Front Pay Loss				191,590
Back Pay plus Front Pay				351,993

Jury Instructions

1. The court will now instruct you as to the claims and defenses of each party and the law governing the case. Please pay close attention to these instructions. You must arrive at your verdict by applying the law as you are now instructed to the facts as you find them.
2. The parties to this case are Mary Anne Williams, the Plaintiff, and David A. Simonson, Christine Jefferson, Nita University, and The Patterson Institute, the codefendants. Ms. Williams has sued the defendants, seeking to recover damages based on a number of claims.
   a. First, Ms. Williams claims that the defendants discriminated against her on the basis of her gender.

On this gender discrimination claim, the plaintiff, Ms. Williams, has the burden of proving, by a preponderance of the evidence, a prima facie case of discrimination. To do so, she must show:

(1) she belongs to a protected class, i.e. she is a female,

(2) Plaintiff worked for Defendant Nita University commencing in YR-8, until her employment was terminated in YR-2. Ms. Williams was qualified and eligible for tenurial status with the School of Public Policy of the Defendant Nita University pursuant to the regulations of Defendant Nita University. Plaintiff should have received tenurial status as a result of a positive vote for her tenure from the tenurial faculty of the Defendant Nita University; and

(3) Ms. Williams was not granted tenure status by the Defendant Nita University, despite the positive vote from the tenurial faculty, while a male professor with a lower academic rank and less qualifications was recommended for and granted tenure by the Defendant Nita University; or

(4) Ms. Williams was not recommended for tenure by the Defendant Jefferson by whom she was supervised during her employment at the Defendant Nita University in retaliation for the Plaintiff terminating a sexual relationship with Defendant Simonson during her time of employment at the Defendant Patterson Institute.

In order to prevail on this claim, the Plaintiff, Ms. Williams, must prove by a preponderance of the evidence, that: (1) she was a female and an employee of the defendant(s), (2) she was subjected to sexual harassment in the form of unwelcome sexual advances or requests for sexual favors, (3) the harassment complained of was based on sex, and (4) her submission to the unwelcome advances was an express or implied condition for receiving job benefits or that her refusal to submit to a supervisor's sexual demands resulted in tangible job detriment.

Or, Ms. Williams must prove by a preponderance of the evidence, that (1) she was female and an employee of the defendant; (2) that she ended a voluntary sexual relationship with the defendant Simonson; (3) that in retaliation for her actions, the defendant Nita University denied her tenurial status and terminated her as its employee.

   b. Second, the plaintiff, Ms. Williams, claims that the defendant(s) committed the act of gender discrimination by creating a "hostile working environment."

In order to prevail on this "hostile working environment" claim, the plaintiff, Ms. Williams, must prove: (1) she was an employee and a member of a protected class, i.e. a female, (2) she was subjected to an unwelcome and hostile work environment in that her employers, Nita University and The Patterson Institute, encouraged and/or allowed sexual relationships between women employees and their male supervisors who were in a position to affect the working conditions of the women employees thereby creating conditions of employment so severe or pervasive as to alter the conditions of Ms. Williams's employment and create an abusive working environment.

If Ms. Williams succeeds in proving the prima facie case of gender discrimination or hostile work environment, the burden shifts to the defendant(s) to articulate some legitimate, non-discriminatory reason for Ms. Williams not being granted tenure.

Should the defendant(s) meet the burden of articulating a legitimate, non-discriminatory reason for rejecting Ms. Williams tenurial status, the Plaintiff must then prove, by a preponderance of the evidence, that the reasons offered by the defendant(s) were not the true reasons for her rejection, but rather a pretext for discrimination.

   c. Third, the plaintiff, Ms. Williams claims that the defendant(s) intentionally inflicted emotional distress:
      (1) for the specific purpose of causing serious mental distress requiring professional psychological and medical intervention.
      (2) The actions and omissions of Defendant Nita University in ratifying the acts of Defendant Jefferson and Defendant Simonson were malicious, willful, wanton, outrageous in the extreme, and intolerable in a civilized society.
   d. Fourth, the plaintiff, Ms. Williams, was wrongfully terminated from her employment at Defendant Nita University and Defendant The Patterson Institute by the defendant(s).

3. If you find that Ms. Williams has proved any or all of the above claims, you may award damages as follows:
   a. Award Ms. Williams the amount of money in wages and fringe benefits that you determine Ms. Williams lost in the past and/or will lose in the future as a result of defendant(s)' unlawful conduct.
   b. Award Ms. Williams the amount of money that fairly compensates her for any mental pain and anguish, embarrassment, humiliation, and loss of any of the joys of life that you find have been cause by the defendants.
   c. If you find that Ms. Williams has proved none of the gender discrimination claims, you will render a verdict for the defendant(s) and award no damages.
4. In addition to the above-mentioned claims of gender discrimination, Ms. Williams also has sued the defendant(s), seeking to recover damages for the tort of defamation. Ms. Williams claims that following her employment termination, the plaintiff applied for positions on the faculty of other universities, including Columbus University and Nita State University, during which time Defendant Simonson and Defendant Jefferson, director of the Defendant Patterson Institute and dean of the school of public policy, respectively, provided statements about the Plaintiff in letters to the aforementioned institutions from which the Plaintiff had sought employment.

(1) These statements were false and slanderous with regard to the Plaintiff's professional qualifications and were issued with the express, implied, or apparent authority of the Defendant Patterson Institute and thereby ratified by the Defendant Patterson Institute

(2) These statements were false and slanderous with regard to the Plaintiff's professional qualifications and were issued with the express, implied, or apparent authority of the Defendant Nita University and thereby ratified by the Defendant Nita University.

(3) As a result of these aforementioned statements and ratifications by the Defendant Nita University and Defendant The Patterson Institute, Plaintiff has suffered substantial emotional distress, mental anguish, and pain and suffering as well as damage to her personal and professional reputation and earning capacity.

In order to prevail on her claim of defamation, the plaintiff, Ms. Williams, must prove, by a preponderance of the evidence, that the defendant(s) published at least one statement which defamed her, causing her harm.

"Publication" means that the defendant(s) communicated by speaking or writing an idea to some other person.

A communication is "defamatory" if, taken as a whole, it tends to harm the reputation of the victim as to lower her in the estimation of the community or to deter a third party from associating or dealing with her.

If you find that the communication, even if it was defamatory of the plaintiff, was substantially true, you will return a verdict in favor of the defendant(s) and against the plaintiff.

If you find that the defendant(s)' communication was defamatory, but was made subject to a conditional privilege, then you must find for the defendant(s) unless the plaintiff proves that the privilege was abused by the defendant(s) in that they acted knowingly, recklessly or maliciously.

In this case, I find and instruct you a conditional privilege applies. This privilege conditionally protects statements made where the publisher(s) of the statement (the defendant(s)) reasonably believe(s) that he or she is protecting the interest of the recipient of the statement or a person who may act on the defamatory statement. For example, the conditional statement extends to statements of reference made by an employer about a present or past employee to a prospective employer. Thus, the references provided by Defendant Simonson and Defendant Jefferson to Mary Anne Williams's prospective employers are within the protection of the conditional privilege.

However, you shall find that the defendant(s) lost the protection of the privilege if the plaintiff proves, by a preponderance of the evidence, that the defendant(s) defamed her with knowledge of its falsity, recklessly (that is, without regard to whether it was true or false), or intentionally.

If you find that the defendant(s) are liable for defamation, the plaintiff is entitled to be fairly and adequately compensated for all harm she suffered as a result of the defamatory communications published by the defendant(s). The injuries for which you may compensate the plaintiff by an award of damages against the defendant(s) include:

a. the actual harm to the plaintiff's reputation which you find resulted from the defendant(s) conduct, and

b. the emotional distress, mental anguish, and humiliation which you find the plaintiff suffered as a result of the defendant(s)' conduct (as well as the bodily harm which you find was caused by such suffering).

5. Special Instruction on Agency.

A principal is liable for the acts of its agent if the agent is liable, where: (1) a principal-agent relationship exists, and (2) the agent performs the acts for which he is liable while acting within the scope of his employment and in furtherance of the principal's business. If you find that the defendants Simonson and Jefferson were acting as the agents of the Defendant Nita University, then their conduct is imputable to the Defendant Nita University. If you find that the acts of the Defendant Simonson was acting as the agent of the Defendant The Patterson Institute, then their conduct is imputable to the defendant Nita University.

IN THE UNITED STATES DISTRICT COURT
FOR THE DISTRICT OF NITA

MARY ANNE WILLIAMS Plaintiff v. DAVID A. SIMONSON, CHRISTINE JEFFERSON, NITA UNIVERSITY, and THE PATTERSON INSTITUTE Defendants	: : : : : : : : : : :	CIVIL ACTION NO. YR-1-1-1414 JURY TRIAL DEMANDED:

4. On her claim of defamation______________________________

SPECIAL VERDICT FORM

We, the jury, and each of us, finds:

1. (a) On her claim of gender discrimination for the Plaintiff:
   and against the defendant(s):
   - i. Defendant Simonson yes_____ no_____
     in the amount of $_________________________
   - ii. Defendant Jefferson yes_____ no_____
     in the amount of $_________________________
   - iii. Defendant Nita University yes_____ no_____
     in the amount of $_________________________
   - iv. Defendant Patterson Institute yes_____ no_____
     in the amount of $_________________________.

   (b) On her claim of gender discrimination:
   and for the defendant(s):
   - i.. Defendant Simonson yes_____ no_____
   - ii. Defendant Jefferson yes_____ no_____
   - iii. Defendant Nita University yes_____ no_____
   - iv. Defendant Patterson Institute yes_____ no_____

(Answer either 1(a) or 1(b)

2. (a) On her claim of intentional infliction of emotional distress: and against the defendant(s):
   - i. Defendant Simonson yes_____ no_____
     in the amount of $_________________________
   - ii. Defendant Jefferson yes_____ no_____
     in the amount of $_________________________
   - iii. Defendant Nita University yes_____ no_____
     in the amount of $_________________________
   - iv. Defendant Patterson Institute yes_____ no_____
     in the amount of $_________________________.

   (b) On her claim of intentional infliction of emotional distress: and for the defendant(s):
   - i. Defendant Simonson yes_____ no_____
   - ii. Defendant Jefferson yes_____ no_____
   - iii. Defendant Nita University yes_____ no_____
   - iv. Defendant Patterson Institute yes_____ no_____

(Answer either Question 2(a) or 2(b).)

3. (a) On her claim of wrongful termination: and against the defendant(s):
   - i. Defendant Simonson yes_____ no_____
     in the amount of $_________________________
   - ii. Defendant Jefferson yes_____ no_____
     in the amount of $_________________________
   - iii. Defendant Nita University yes_____ no_____
     in the amount of $_________________________
   - iv. Defendant Patterson Institute yes_____ no_____
     in the amount of $_________________________.

   (b) On her claim of wrongful termination: and for the defendant(s):
   - i. Defendant Simonson yes_____ no_____
   - ii. Defendant Jefferson yes_____ no_____
   - iii. Defendant Nita University yes_____ no_____
   - iv. Defendant Patterson Institute yes_____ no_____

(Answer either Question 3(a) or 3(b).)

4. (a) On her claim of defamation:
   and against the defendant(s):
   i. Defendant Simonson yes_____ no_____
   in the amount of $________________________
   ii. Defendant Jefferson yes_____ no_____
   in the amount of $________________________
   iii. Defendant Nita University yes_____ no_____
   in the amount of $________________________
   iv. Defendant Patterson Institute yes_____ no_____
   in the amount of $________________________.

   (b) On her claim of defamation:
   and for the defendant(s):
   i. Defendant Simonson yes_____ no_____
   ii. Defendant Jefferson yes_____ no_____
   iii. Defendant Nita University yes_____ no_____
   iv. Defendant Patterson Institute yes_____ no_____

(Answer either Question 4(a) or 4(b).)

____

Foreperson